Betty Cornell's Teen-Age Popularity Guide

BETTY CORNELL'S TEEN-AGE POPULARITY GUIDE

Illustrated by ABBI DAMEROW

PENGUIN BOOKS

PENGUIN BOOKS

Published by the Penguin Group
Penguin Books Ltd, 80 Strand, London WC2R 0RL, England
Penguin Group (USA) LLC, 375 Hudson Street, New York, New York 10014, USA
Penguin Group (Canada), 90 Eglinton Avenue East, Suite 700, Toronto, Ontario, Canada M4P 2Y3
(a division of Pearson Penguin Canada Inc.)
Penguin Ireland, 25 St Stephen's Green, Dublin 2, Ireland (a division of Penguin Books Ltd)
Penguin Group (Australia), 707 Collins Street, Melbourne, Victoria 3008, Australia
(a division of Pearson Australia Group Pty Ltd)
Penguin Books India Pvt Ltd, 11 Community Centre, Panchsheel Park, New Delhi – 110 017, India
Penguin Group (NZ), 67 Apollo Drive, Rosedale, Auckland 0632, New Zealand
(a division of Pearson New Zealand Ltd)
Penguin Books (South Africa) (Pty) Ltd, Block D, Rosebank Office Park, 181 Jan Smuts Avenue,
Parktown North, Gauteng 2193, South Africa

Penguin Books Ltd, Registered Offices: 80 Strand, London WC2R 0RL, England

penguin.com

This edition published in the USA by Dutton Books, an imprint of Penguin Group (USA) LLC, 2014
Published simultaneously in Great Britain by Penguin Books 2014
001

Copyright © Prentice-Hall, Inc., 1953
Copyright © renewed by Betty Cornell Huston, 1981
Portions of this work appeared in *Betty Cornell's Glamour Guide for Teens* (Prentice-Hall, 1951)
Foreword copyright © Maya Van Wagenen, 2014
All rights reserved

The moral right of the copyright holders has been asserted

Printed in Italy by Graphicom

British Library Cataloguing in Publication Data
A CIP catalogue record for this book is available from the British Library

ISBN: 978–0–141–35595–5

A note of thanks to Helen Carlton, Steve Elliot, and Dr. Edward Hymes for their wonderful help.

BETTY CORNELL

Foreword

I believe in fate.

Not everyone does, but after what I've experienced because of the book in your hands, I would be crazy not to. This book found my dad years before I was born. I can imagine it, sitting on a cluttered bookshelf at a thrift store, no dust jacket, just a faded, torn, blue cover, and a spine that read the name in bold red letters: BETTY CORNELL'S TEEN-AGE POPULARITY GUIDE. I can picture my father, the history-professor-to-be, pulling it from its spot on the shelf where it had been sitting, wait-

ing for who knows how long. He brought it home, lugged it around with him on his various moves, and kept it on the bookshelf in his office as a piece of vintage pop culture. He almost got rid of it many times, but never got around to it.

And then the book found me. It was the summer before eighth grade when it was pulled out of a box in Dad's office. I saw it, picked it up, and met Betty Cornell.

By following Betty's advice on popularity that school year, I found out more about myself and others than I ever

thought possible. This book taught me about everything from girdles, hair, and makeup to bravery, self-confidence, and the importance of reaching out to others. The funny, blunt, and helpful advice that fills each page made Betty feel like the older sister I never had. I admired her, blamed her when things didn't go exactly to plan, and had long conversations in my head with the teen-model-turned-author who was so sure of herself and so sure of me and my abilities to overcome my fears and better myself. She gave me pep talks, pushed me out of my comfort zone, then watched proudly from the sidelines when I finally found my wings and learned to fly.

When I met Betty Cornell in person a year after the experiment, it was as if I had known her for a long time. That smile I saw on her face when I gave her a hug was the same as the one that greeted me on that first page when I cracked open the cover. Everything she said was an echo of her book, and it was clear that she had written what she believed, what came from her heart and stuck with her all those years.

Betty changed my life and shaped the person I am today. Fate led her book to me at the time when I needed her most.

And maybe it's through fate that she's found you.

So go ahead, introduce yourself. You're in for one amazing ride.

MAYA VAN WAGENEN
Author of *Popular: Vintage Wisdom for a Modern Geek*

Contents

Betty Cornell's
Teen-Age
Popularity
Guide

1

Introduction

"Hi!"

I'm Betty Cornell. I'm the author of this book and I think it only fair to tell you how I got to be that way. First of all let me say that I don't consider myself any great shakes as far as being an author goes. I'm not a writer. I'm a model. But the truth of the matter is that because I am a model I decided to write this book.

I wrote this book to set down for you the things I learned about beauty and popularity from being a model—the know-how and the how and the why, etc. Also I have tried to answer the questions teen-agers have kept asking me, such as

"What do I say?" "What do I do?" "How do I act in such and such a situation?"

The answers I've given here are based on my own personal experience. Being a model, I had to know what was the right thing to say and do any time, anywhere. A model is so much in the limelight that she just can't afford to make mistakes. Believe me, when you're on parade all day long, you learn fast. You smooth off your rough edges in a hurry.

In the process of smoothing off rough edges, you find yourself in no time at all what people call "Polished." Suddenly you're the kind of person who does the right thing naturally and easily at all times. You have that wonderful and elusive thing called poise. The girl with poise is the girl who knows about good personal care and good conduct. She may not be the prettiest girl, but she's certainly one of the most popular. She gets the dates, the class offices, the bids to college proms.

Because I learned all these basics while I was a teen-ager, I hope that you as teen-agers will find my suggestions helpful. They are specifically designed for you, not for your mothers or your grandmothers, although I wouldn't be surprised if you find that older people are borrowing this book of yours from time to time.

The purpose of my book, then, is to help you teen-agers make the most of yourselves. If you follow through on what I have written here, I know you will be pleased with the results. I say so because these are the methods by which I made myself over from a chubby and awkward little high-school girl into a full-fledged model. Just to prove that I'm not fooling, that I mean what I say, I'm going to review a little bit of my personal history for you. At the end I think you'll see that the only difference between Betty Cornell, the shy, awkward, tubby teen, and Betty Cornell, the model, is the difference between a girl who just slopped along and a girl who found out how to look and act her best.

Not so very long ago, when I was fifteen years old, I was doing all the things any ordinary teen-ager does. I was living with my family, going to school, and being the bane of my older brother Bob's existence. I thought I knew everything. Bob knew that I didn't, and was always trying to prove it.

I remember that one of my biggest problems was the fact that Bob used to rule my social life with an iron hand. He would come to parties where I was having a gay time, ring the doorbell, and announce: "Come to pick up my sister. Time for her to go home." Then I was mortified. Now I realize that he was doing the right thing.

In fact, I know now that an older brother is about the best social insurance any teen-ager can have. I found that Bob was the best person to tell me what the score was as far as boys were concerned. Lots of the tips on boys that I have included in some of the chapters of this

book were tips I first learned from him.

It was then, when I was fifteen, coping with brother Bob and living in Teaneck, New Jersey, a small suburban community not far from New York City, that I decided to become a model. As a matter of fact, I didn't make the decision myself; a friend of my mother's did. I was casting about for a way to earn money for college and, being young and unknowing, I decided to try my luck.

And it was luck. I was accepted as a model, but not for glamorous poses. My early modeling consisted of posing for tubby teen pictures. I soon learned there was not much future in being a tubby teen. So at sixteen I took stock of my situation and decided to really go to work on myself.

I did all the things that you will read about later in this book. I went on a sensible diet, cut out between-meal nibbling (I used to eat enough between meals to satisfy an army), did daily exercises, cleared up my complexion, and styled my hair. And with the help of my family, including Bob, and the advice of my friends and fellow-models, I learned how best to cope with the social situations that came up in both my private and my professional life. At the end of my self-improvement campaign, I was no longer a tubby teen in every sense of the term, I was a real junior-size model with a lot of self-confidence.

In fact my campaign was such a success that when I graduated from high school I found that I did not have enough time between modeling jobs to keep up my college work. So I devoted myself exclusively to modeling. I have never regretted giving up college, for I went on so many trips to Arizona, to Florida, and to Canada as a model, that traveling became an education in itself.

As you know, I'm still modeling today. And I still keep right on performing all the simple rituals outlined for you here. Now I don't guarantee that these rituals will make you a model, or the most popular girl in your town. But I do guarantee that they will make you prettier and happier. I point out to you that these routines made me a model, just in order to give you confidence in my suggestions, to prove to you that they really, truly work.

I know teen-agers who have tried my suggestions and I know with what good results. Some time ago I gave a series of lectures in the Youth Center in my home town of Teaneck. It is from that series of lectures that this book has grown. Here, as in those lectures, all I have tried to do is make suggestions. The rest is up to you. Suggestions aren't good if they're not put into practice. I hope you'll find that putting them into practice is lots of fun. I did.

The reason I say it's fun is that every girl, I don't care who she may be, wants to be attractive and popular. To get to be that kind of girl, all you have to do is try some of my suggestions. They work. What I did, you can do too. I found that the best way to tackle the job is to recognize that success is up to *you*. If you put real elbow grease into acquiring beauty, poise and polish, you'll find it pays off with more dates, more fun, more good times. Gee, what more could anyone ask?

2

Figure Problems

"I'm too fat."

"I'm too thin."

Nearly every teen has had one of these figure problems at one time or another in her life. As a matter of fact, some teens have probably had both within the space of a semester or so. The reason this is so is that as a teen-ager your body is still in a state of flux—it has not stopped growing long enough to find its natural balance.

Your body does not competely finish growing until you reach the age of twenty-one or so. Of course, by the time you reach your teens you have stopped growing as rapidly as a baby, but you are still growing nonetheless—if you have stopped growing up, you have started growing out, or vice versa.

But just because your body is restless and refuses to settle down is no reason to despair of having a good figure. It is a question of mind over matter. Start by intelligently figuring out your figure problem. Find out about your body. Are you large-boned or small-boned? Is your tendency toward longness and leanness or to shortness and plumpness? Stand before your mirror and contemplate yourself from head to toe. Fish out the measuring tape and take statistics.

Statistics are alarmingly accurate. Chances are when you take yours you will wish they weren't so. Those extra pounds that you guessed you might have gained are unequivocally recorded on the tape measure. What you feared has come to pass, what a popped button or a pulled seam has been plainly insinuating for some time, is true: you are overweight.

Now overweight is nothing to be alarmed about. It is easy enough to do something about it and do something about it sensibly. Don't lose your head and go on a starvation diet. First talk the matter over intelligently with your family and your doctor. It may be that your extra pounds have come about because of a glandular disturbance. It is more probable that they are a result of overeating. But never take the chance of upsetting your body routine by a silly diet. Always check first with your doctor before you make any plans to lose weight. When you get his O.K., then and only then diet, and diet under his supervision.

When you are dieting, stick to your doctor's advice as to what your proper weight should be. When you reach the figure he has set for you, stop there. Don't try to become underweight on the assumption that you will look more glamorous when you are thin, pale and wan. 'Tain't so. You won't look glamorous at all—just bedraggled and tired out.

Another important thing to remember about a diet is that it is just as important to count the calories you eat between meals as the ones you eat at meals. In fact, many of you would probably not need to diet if you cut down your between-meal nibbling.

Have you ever stopped to add up all those extra snacks you tuck away during the day? A bar of chocolate at recess, Coke and pretzels in the drugstore after school, peanut butter and jelly sandwiches before dinner, and before bed all the leftovers from dinner. When you stop and think about it, all those tidbits add up to quite a sum.

What's more, that's not all the between-meal nibbling that goes on. There is still to be considered all the gorging that takes place at parties, particularly at club meetings and general get-togethers. I am being fair, I think, when I assume that many of you stuff away a good bit of

the following: peanuts, crackers, potato chips, carbonated beverages, and finally a helping of some large, lush pastry.

I speak of in-between eating so forcefully because it's just that kind of eating, a nibble here and a nibble there all day long, that was my Waterloo. In fact, in high school I was renowned for being able to stow away more than any other girl in the crowd. Boys who took me out on a date suffered in their budgets for weeks afterwards. I wasn't just a one-hamburger girl—I was a two- or three-hamburger terror. Need I add that for a time my dates were few and far between?

So I say that if you are worried about your weight, cut down between-meal nibbling. Pass up the party fare and concentrate on eating your fill at mealtime. That's what meals are for.

There is one meal in particular that should not be overlooked—and that meal is breakfast. Now, there are some teens who think that skipping breakfast keeps the weight down. Such, I am sad to relate, is not the case. Non-breakfast-eaters too often find that hunger drives them to nibbling before lunch and nibbling on things that are loaded with calories: things like chocolate, cookies, and pastry.

No, if you are serious about having a good figure you must eat breakfast. I eat a good, substantial breakfast every day. I eat it because I found out that it is the most important meal of the day. It is the meal when your body, after an all-night fast, needs food and is better able to assimilate what it takes in.

If you are one of those Lazy Lils who just can't get up in time to eat breakfast, then you are starting the day off on the wrong foot. If you call downstairs: "Just five more minutes, Mother," then you had better plan your evenings more systematically so that you get to bed early enough

to make you feel rested and raring to go come morning.

Eating a good breakfast may not come easily at first. But after a little practice you'll find you enjoy it. I know I do. And you'll feel much better for doing so. You'll have more pep and more energy, and if you stick to the menus I am about to suggest, you'll also have less poundage.

SAMPLE BREAKFAST MENUS

1

1 half grapefruit
1 soft-boiled egg
1 slice whole-wheat or rye toast (use small amount of butter)
1 glass of milk
Coffee or tea (if Mom allows it), but drink it black, no cream or sugar.

2

Orange juice
Ready-to-eat cereal with milk (½ cup) and one teaspoon sugar—no more than that (I saw you reach again for the sugar bowl. Put it back, you'll learn to do with less.)
1 glass of milk
Coffee (black) or tea

3

1 half grapefruit
1 poached egg on rye or whole-wheat toast, small amount of butter
1 glass of milk

4

Sliced orange
Hot cereal, ¾ cup of milk, one teaspoon of sugar
1 slice of toast (and watch that butter)
1 glass of milk

These suggested menus are not something dreamed up for this book. They are the result of many years of expert study by people who know what they are talking about, the dietitians. And these diets work. I know: I use them.

There are just a few things I want to note about these menus. One is the absence of any kind of fried food. That is because fried food of any sort is fattening. If you persist in sticking to your favorite sunny-sides-up, your day of reckoning will come. You will be forced to choose between letting out all your waistbands or buying a new school skirt with the money you were saving for a formal.

The other point I want to mention about these menus is the alternating of eggs and cereal. That is done to keep breakfast from becoming monotonous. If you vary your low-calorie dishes, you will tend to forget that you are even on a diet.

After breakfast comes lunch. I don't have to ask what you have been eating at that time of day because I remember what I used to pack away—a meal that would have done justice to a football player. It wasn't long, either, before I began to look like one of the team's tackles.

Many of you bring your lunches to school and buy milk at the cafeteria. That is a good way to avoid temptation—you don't even have to go near the long line of delicious dishes. With a little coopera-

tion from your mother, you can plan to bring a non-fattening and nutritious luncheon. Here are a few ideas about what to pack:

1. Hard-boiled eggs.
2. Small container of cottage cheese.
3. One slice of whole-wheat or rye bread —small amount of butter.
4. Fresh fruit (you can eat lots of it).
5. American or Swiss cheese sandwich, lots of lettuce—no mayonnaise— use whole-wheat or rye bread.
6. Any kind of lean-meat sandwich.
7. Consommé.
8. MILK.

Any sensible combination of three or four of these items will make a healthful luncheon and one that is light and easy to carry. Probably the only difference between what I have listed and the lunch you are accustomed to packing is the absence here of cake and cookies. But just because they are absent, don't think that you can slip into line and get a few. Oh no, the desserts were left out on purpose. If the prospect of lunch without a sweet dessert is too gruesome for you to imagine, there's no hope for you. You have allowed your sweet tooth to overrule your wisdom tooth.

On the other hand, there are those of

FRIED EGGS? OR NEW FORMAL?

you who bring money to school instead of a lunch-box. You are in a more dangerous position than your lunch-toting friends who turn their backs on the rows of food and can concentrate on hard-boiled eggs. You must go down the line of jelly doughnuts, chocolate cakes, peanut butter sandwiches and such. But stand firm, scoot past these calories, and plant yourself in front of the salads.

Choose from any of the salads, but pay particular attention to the leafy green ones, the vegetable concoctions, and the fruit fantasies. These will be the best for you, because you can push the dressing to one side. Salad dressings, both French and mayonnaise, are taboo for dieters because they are rich and oily. Salads such as chicken, avocado, and tuna fish are not recommended because they contain food oils as well as dressing oils. One of the best choices you can make is hard-boiled egg garnished with water cress—it is chock full of protein that will help to burn up your excess fat.

After your salad has been selected you may add a slice of bread, rye or whole-wheat, and a glass of milk—white, not chocolate. Then for dessert, sublimate your yearnings for that sumptuous affair of gooey sauce and ice cream and choose from the fruits—either a stewed fruit or a

fresh one. You can vary your selections from day to day, but stick within the suggestions I have outlined for you.

Time for dinner, and all of you, whether you be the lunch toters or the lunch buyers, are beset by the same problem. At breakfast and luncheon you are pretty much on your own; you can easily skip the calories because your choice is varied and what you eat does not conflict with anyone around you. At dinner you are in a different position. Dinner is a family meal. And it is a meal at which the family expects to eat well. Your father looks foward to pie, your mother makes pie.

You cannot expect the rest of the family to give up their pie because you are on a diet. You cannot quarrel with your mother because you refuse to come to the table, afraid that you will succumb to eating that pie if it is offered to you. What you must do is to come to dinner prepared to say nicely, "No, thank you." "No, thank you, no pie. No, thank you, no seconds." In the beginning, you serve yourself and you use no gravy or butter. You indulge yourself with large servings of the green vegetables and you look the other way when the bread is passed. In other words, you eat the meat, the vegetables, the salad. You also may eat the

dessert, but only if it is fruit, Jello without whipped cream, or custard. All through the dinner you keep a careful check on your calories, but you do so without calling attention to the fact. Above all, you join in the family circle, and under no circumstances do you behave like a martyr.

Below I have listed some good non-fattening dinner menus. They will all look familiar because they are just like any normal family dinner with the extras removed.

DINNER ON A DIET

1

1 glass of tomato juice
large patty lean ground beef, broiled, no gravy
large serving of spinach
tomato, lettuce, and hard-cooked egg salad, with vinegar
stewed apricots
1 glass of milk
coffee or tea, if desired or allowed.

2

1 cup clear soup
large patty of ground beef
½ cup boiled cabbage
asparagus salad with sliced tomatoes
small sherbet
1 glass of milk

3

1 cup vegetable soup
veal cutlet, broiled, with the fat removed
½ cup boiled rice, with tablespoon gravy
tomato and cucumber salad, vinegar or lemon juice
1 glass of milk

4

1 glass of tomato juice
generous serving of lean roast beef
small baked potato, ½ teaspoon butter or tablespoon pan gravy
large serving of green leafy vegetable, any kind
3 stalks of celery stuffed with cottage cheese
baked custard
1 glass of milk

5

1 cup vegetable soup
generous serving of lean broiled fish, with lemon
½ cup stewed tomatoes
3 stalks of celery
an apple, pear or any other fresh fruit
1 glass of milk

6

1 glass of tomato juice
generous serving of broiled calf's liver
serving of cooked carrots

tomato and lettuce salad with lemon juice
fruit Jello
1 glass of milk

7

1 cup clear consommé
generous serving of lean roast lamb, beef
    or veal
small serving of mashed potato, with ta-
    blespoon pan gravy
1 cup string beans
tomato and lettuce salad, with vinegar
    dressing
small serving of fruit sherbet
1 glass of milk

If you stick to the three meals a day that have been outlined for you in this chapter, you'll lose weight. Do not be discouraged if nothing happens immediately. A diet that progresses slowly progresses more surely. Trick diets in which you lose weight quickly often turn out to be ones in which all the weight comes right back the minute you stop dieting. Starvation diets such as the all-liquid ones or others popular from time to time can be injurious to the health and should be avoided.

These sample menus give you the proper nutrition and a balanced diet. They will provide you with the correct amount of energy. Still, many of you will feel hungry between meals. What to eat then becomes a problem. It is a great temptation to smuggle a sandwich or a cookie, but try not to do it. Instead nibble on a carrot, finish a leftover custard or munch on an apple. Drink milk or to-mato juice if you are thirsty. As for taunts from your friends—and they will taunt you—keep your chin up and your weight down.

Now for you thin gals who have been patiently waiting while your chubbier friends have been guided over the bumps. Your problem is just as acute. Your bones jut out every which way every time you put on an evening dress, and you feel foolish in a bathing suit. You try to gain weight, but you don't seem to succeed. Perhaps you're going about it the wrong way. Be systematic. Make certain to butter your toast liberally, step up your servings at mealtime—try double portions—and help yourself to lots of dressing and gravy. Take time to eat. Don't rush through meals and don't skip a course.

Get acquainted with calories. Chances are you have been steering away from them. If you don't know what foods are fattening, ask your chubby friends, because they *will* know. The strange irony of the whole figure problem is that so often it is the thin girls who don't drink the double malted milks, while the chubbies just dote on them. Well, it's time to switch places—swing your partner and dos-à-dos.

One warning to girls trying to gain weight is this: do not go overboard on chocolate and very heavy pastries. Though you may gain weight on this type of eating, you will also wreck your complexion. Build up your calorie quota on foods like potatoes, butter, milk products, and sugars. Be sure to nibble between meals, and not on carrot sticks like your

unhappier sisters, but on peanut-butter-and-jelly concoctions. And, most important of all, if you are really underweight, see your doctor. He will be able to prescribe for your best advantage.

Now that the fat girls are thin and the thin ones fat, some advice about striking the happy medium. The happy medium is that weight which best fits your height and your bone structure. It differs for everyone. You and your doctor will be the best judges of that weight, because you'll achieve it when you feel your best and when your mirror tells you that you look your best. Your best weight will be the one at which you can be peppy all day, ready to go anywhere and do anything. If you feel listless and all tired out, chances are that you are not in a healthy condition. To look your best you've got to feel your best, and to do that you must be healthy.

Eating the right food has a lot to do with being healthy. To stay in the groove where your figure likes to be, remember to eat wisely and well. Here's the list of basic foods you need every day so that your body gets its necessary daily requirements of vitamins, minerals, carbohydrates, fats, starches and calories: One quart of milk—that equals one glass at each meal, plus one extra; a serving of whole-grained cereal; an egg a day (not less than five a week); two green vegetables and a green salad; two kinds of fruit, one citrus; a serving of meat, fish or poultry; about three pats of butter; four slices of wholewheat or enriched bread; and lastly, a potato.

There is a lot of food for thought in this chapter. It is full of admonitions to do this and don't do that. Pick and choose and find the suggestions that fit you best. However, don't get too rigid about selections. If you have got your figure in shape, then relax once in a while. Do not apply diet restrictions on any big eating holiday like Christmas or Thanksgiving. If

you do, you'll find that you are taking too much enjoyment out of your life. The thing to do is to be sensible.

If you are sensible you will sample a bit of this or that at a party—that's why the food is there. But you won't sit all evening by the potato chips, one hand in the bowl, the other popping a fresh one in your mouth. If you are sensible, you'll drink Coke and eat peanut butter sandwiches on a picnic, but you will also make sure that you don't chose those very same items next day for lunch. If you are sensible you'll share a soda with your date once in a while, but you won't ask for another and another and another.

In fact, if you are sensible, you won't have any figure problems. You'll watch yourself and catch any bulges or depressions before they have a chance to multiply. You'll be sure to see your doctor for regular check-ups so that you can be full of the old pep in order to live to the fullest the busy life that a good figure combined with a good personality gets a sensible girl.

At the end of the book (pages 125 and 133) you'll find an outline of some good figure improvement exercises, and also a helpful calorie chart.

3

Skin Problems

"My skin always breaks out."
"Mine's too oily."
"Mine's too dry."

It is a lamentable paradox that as babies we nearly all have perfect skins (at a time when it really does us little good), but as teen-agers most of us are beset with one kind of a complexion problem or another. It seems a cruel state of affairs, but it is not one that has to be put up with.

I know that there are teens who think they have to be stuck with splotchy skins, just as I know there are teens who think that "baby fat" is a phase they have to live through. But both are wrong. It's just as true that teens can clear up their complexions by a routine of logical skin care as it is that teens can get rid of tubby tummies by cutting down on calories.

The two big troublemakers in skin conditions are diet and dirt. Too much chocolate and too little soap and water are the basic irritants. A program that banishes these two factors will launch any girl well on the way toward a clear and camellia-like complexion.

In the previous chapter on diet, I pointed out how important to your figure it is to eat sensibly. Well, it is just as important to your skin. A jelly doughnut will not only add pounds, it will also promote pimples. The food you eat every day will affect your complexion every bit as much as it affects your waistline.

If you stick to the daily allotments of food that were suggested to you before, you will be laying the groundwork for a good glowing skin. By eating the necessary amounts of green vegetables and fresh fruits and by lowering your intake of sticky sweets and greasy fried foods you will be doing two good turns: one to your face, the other to your figure.

Even serious skin conditions like acne can be aided by proper diet. Acne, of course, must be treated by a doctor, since it involves more knowledge than any layman has. No teen-ager should take it upon herself to fool around with acne. But a teen-ager who is so disturbed will find that one of the first things a doctor will tell her to do is to keep a careful check on what she eats. If diet can help acne, think how much it can do for the ordinary, commonplace garden variety of skin eruptions.

Stated broadly, a good complexion demands absolute cleanliness. This cleanliness can be divided into two parts: inner and outer. Inner cleanliness is what is gained from proper eating habits. It means that your body is healthy and functioning well. It means that you are free of constipation (which is the ruin of a good skin). Outer cleanliness is what is gained from the vigorous application of soap and water. And the plain truth of the matter is that in this regard some teen-agers are slackers.

It is surprising how few of us realize how essential it is to clean our skin thoroughly. We give a few swipes with the soap and we're done with it. Some of us, indeed, hardly even bother with the soap, and others (lost souls) bother with nothing at all. They even apply fresh makeup over the remains of the old.

No skin will stand up under such treatment. The pores will rebel. Dirt will get clogged up in them and sooner or later blackheads and hickies will start popping forth on all sides.

So if you are campaigning for a petal-smooth complexion, start each day and end each day with a clean skin. When you wash, pin your hair up out of the way so that you will have no scruples about scrubbing right up into the hairline. Before you begin make sure that you have the necessary equipment, a good cleansing cream, a soap that agrees with your skin and water, and a clean washcloth.

First start with the cleansing cream, which you should apply liberally and with upward strokes. Pulling down on the facial tissues will, after a period of time, tend to make the muscles go slack. As you work the cream into the skin, remember that the pressure of your fingertips helps stimulate the circulation of the blood. It is one part of the function of the blood stream, you know, to carry off the body's waste materials. If the circulation is sluggish, the wastes will collect in one spot and manifest themselves in a nasty collection of blotches before you know it.

Make sure, as you rub in the cream, that you spread it over every inch and into the crevices around the nose, mouth, and eyes. Too often these areas are overlooked. If they begin to feel neglected, they will start demanding attention, like a small child who has been left out of the conversation too long. Only instead of setting up a loud wail, they will express their resentment by breaking out or getting wrinkly and dried up.

When you have thoroughly covered your face with cream, allow it to remain on the skin for about two minutes. Just sit back and luxuriate in the cool slippery feeling that it gives. Then gently begin to remove all the cream with a tissue, being careful to sop up every bit. Before you throw away the soiled tissue, take a moment to look at it. Dirty, isn't it? Did you ever guess there was so much grime on your face? See what you've been missing?

The next step in the cleansing routine is to wash your face with soap and water. Use hot water for the soaping. The soap you choose should be one for your skin type— a castile soap for a dry skin, a soap with a drying agent for an oily skin. If you are not certain what to choose, ask your druggist for advice.

After soaping—no skimping there, please—rinse your face with cold water. The cold water will close the pores that have opened up with the application of the hot water. It is important to remember the cold water, since pores should always be closed after cleansing so that new dirt will not have an opportunity to get down deep. Twice a week, use ice cubes in place of the cold water. They do a very thorough job and besides they feel wonderfully slithery.

Use the routine I have outlined twice a

day. It will take time at first until you get in the swing of it, but you will find each minute worth your while. However, you may discover that you are monopolizing the one family bathroom. If so, arrange to schedule your beauty ablutions when the rest of the family has business elsewhere. Get up earlier in the morning if necessary and in the evening start your program before the family is ready to go to bed.

Actually, it is essential to take the time to do a good job. Furthermore, if you faithfully follow all the steps, you will have no need of complicated cosmetics primarily designed for adult skins. When you are a teen-ager, steer clear of tricky

formulas and concentrate on the two fundamental aspects of cleanliness—inner and outer. You will find that these simple routines will be more than adequate to keep your complexion glowing.

There is one note of warning I would like to sound in connection with this question of cleanliness. Keep your washcloth fresh. Scrubbing with a dirty cloth will nullify all your efforts, no matter how heartily you work. Wash your cloth every night and hang it up to dry where it can get the light and air. Do not crush it into a damp little ball and fling it in a corner where it will lie limply until the next time. A dirty cloth will spread germs and might cause infection.

Simple adherence to detail ought to keep any teen-age skin in shape. However, from time to time unfortunate major blemishes do occur. At such time, specific remedies are in order.

Let us suppose that in spite of your best efforts blackheads have begun blossoming. There is no getting around it, for there they are, the little devils. Blackheads are caused by blocked-up pores, clogged with dirt that has not been carefully enough removed from the skin. Oily skins are more susceptible than are dry ones, since dirt clings more stubbornly to an oily skin once it gets a toehold. To get rid of blackheads the remedy is twofold: reduce the oiliness and clean out the pores.

To reduce oiliness, you should, as you remember, be very careful as to your diet. Be sure to avoid rich and greasy foods. To remove dirt, there is nothing to do but to wash and wash and wash. Use very hot water which will steam open the pores (like the dentist who says "Wider, please"). With the pores open, the dirt can be dislodged more readily.

Oftentimes it is necessary to squeeze the blackheads in order to force out the little plugs of dirt. If you do so, squeeze them oh so carefully with your fingers protected by tissue. Warning—never use your bare fingers. Fingernails can cause infection if they are not antiseptically clean. It is far better to take the precaution of using the tissue and not run this risk. After squeezing, rub the skin with ice cubes. As I explained before, they will cause the pores to contract.

Once you have squeezed a blackhead, do not irritate it by picking at it. If an itchy finger starts to wander in the vicinity of your face during study period or during an idle hour when you are listening to the radio, stop it dead in its tracks. You can do immense harm by opening up an irritated skin area with a dirty nail. Infections can be introduced which will really make your skin a problem for the specialist.

Blackheads occur most often at the nose and chin, because those two areas tend to be the most oily and are the most inaccessible for a thorough cleansing job. Keep a close watch over those danger spots. It is easier to prevent a blackhead than it is to cure one.

Permission to squeeze blackheads, it must be understood, does not carry blanket permission to squeeze everything in sight. Hickies must never be squeezed. Unlike blackheads, hickies contain pus, which, if sufficiently irritated, can erupt in even more monstrous form and cause excessive damage to the skin, to say nothing of leaving ugly scars. Hickies should be treated with great respect.

The best treatment is one that dries them up. In the summer the sun will often take care of this for you. Otherwise, there are two preparations which will do the job at anytime of the year. If you have a dry skin, a dab of zinc oxide, which you can buy at any drugstore, will clear them up in short order. If you have an oily skin, a smear of calamine lotion, also available at any drug counter, will do the same. Keep applying these remedies until the hickies have vanished: by no means get impatient and start squeezing.

Whiteheads, although not as large an eyesore as hickies, or as blatantly evident as a blackhead, are nonetheless unpleasant because they mar the smooth surface of the skin. These are caused by sluggish circulation of the blood and niggardly massage. Exercise your fingertips and rub away those little bumps, which only represent lumps of waste material collected under the surface of the skin.

Many times just plain oily skin is the bane of an otherwise good-looking complexion. Somehow the skin never seems quite clean. This condition is sometimes related to changes in the body patterns, but it can be corrected. It is not a phase you have to live through. Proper measures will help counteract it.

In addition to a careful diet I recommend a good cleanser—one that will dig down deep and get out the dirt. I also stress constant washing, not just twice a day, but in between times as well. Say once before lunch and once again after school. It is imperative to remember that you must change your makeup often so that it cannot get rubbed into the pores and clog them up. Never apply new makeup over old if you have an oily skin.

Teens with an oily skin can never scrub too much. Soap and water are their best friends. On the other hand, teens with dry skin should cut down on soap and water and use cream in their place, although they must be just as scrupulous with their cleansing routine. They should use castile soap and water twice a day and a good rich cream in between.

To help along a dry skin, teens so troubled should apply baby oil at night before going to bed. Baby oil is an excellent skin aid. In summer it can be used liberally to counteract exposure to the drying rays of the sun, which cause many skins to shrivel up like prunes. The rest of the year it need not be used quite so freely, but a thin layer of it each night will work wonders.

When it comes to skins that are part oily, part dry, sort of Dr. Jekyll-Mr. Hyde skins, treat your face as if it were more oily than dry. Adhere to the frequent-washing routine outlined previously, and then, to soothe the Sahara areas, swab those spots with a little baby oil.

Some teen-agers complain of mysterious skin afflictions. They have pimples and rashes which do not seem to fall into any of the normal categories. These mysterious blemishes are sometimes caused by unhealthy scalps. If such blemishes break out at the temples, the forehead and at the nape of the neck, the chances are that it is your scalp that is at fault. Proper care of the scalp and hair will be treated in the next chapter, but it is well to point out here and now that the two problems are interrelated.

As a matter of fact, it is worth remembering that no single beauty problem can be isolated from any other. What you eat affects your figure, your skin, and (as you will find out later) your hair and even your nails. How clean you are determines how smooth your skin will be and also how glossy your hair will gleam. In beauty, as in geometry, everything correlates.

In the long run, it is a good thing to have all of your bodily functions so intertwined. It makes your beauty program so much easier. In a sense you are killing several birds with one stone. A salad does a good turn for your face as well as your figure—daily death-to-dirt scrubbing removes grime as well as stimulating circulation.

In actuality, then, beauty is lots more than skin deep. Beauty is as deep as you are. Beauty is all of you, your face, your figure, your skin. More than any other part, though, your skin will be the barometer of your beauty weather. It will tell you how well you are keeping to a beauty schedule. A broken-out complexion is a sure sign that you have slipped up somewhere. It is an indication that you have eaten too many sweets or skimped on cleanliness. Remember to be diligent in your daily habits, and your reward will be a smooth, silken complexion (and, not incidentally, a fine face and figure).

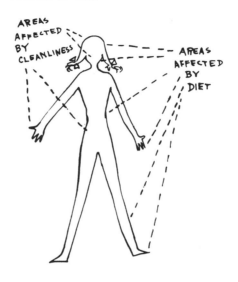

4

Hair

"I can't do a thing with it."

Beautiful hair is about the most important thing a girl has. Whether it be blond, brunette or red, pretty hair can always overcome the handicap of a not-so-pretty face. Unhappily, I must state, the reverse is just as true: unattractive hair can make even the prettiest face seem dull and unattractive. Your hair can make you or break you.

Hair can do all this because hair is what we remember most about a person. How many times have you described a friend as being "that attractive blond" or that

"adorable redhead"? How many times have you observed that the first thing you notice about a stranger is the way she wears her hair? How many times have you been astonished to discover that what seems like an overnight metamorphosis in some friend is simply the result of a change of hair-do?

Because hair is so all-important, no teen-ager should ever let herself get down in the dumps about her own crop. No teen-ager should ever exclaim, "But honestly, I can't do a thing with it!" The truth is that you can do everything with it. Hair is the most manageable attribute that you have.

Hair, unlike a nose or a mouth, can be changed. Hair can be grown or cut. Hair can be curled or left uncurled. It can be pinned up in a topknot or turned loose to the four winds. Hair can be almost anything you want it to be.

The reason I insist that hair can do and be all these things is that I know it can. Hair that is well treated is like a talented fashion model—it responds to direction. In one mood it can look casual, in another it can look chic and sophisticated. As you change your moods, you can change your hair to fit. In fact, you do. You rarely wear your hair to a dance the same way you wear it to a beach picnic or a tennis match.

However, there is unfortunately one pitfall in regard to the maneuverability of hair. You really cannot do anything with lifeless hair. Badly kept, dull hair will not respond to direction no matter how long you fuss with it, pin it up, or take it down. For all the good you accomplish in setting it, you might as well have spent the time in a movie. To be manageable (and beautiful), hair must be healthy.

To be healthy, hair must first of all stem from a healthy body. Here again what you eat affects you, for if you are run down or missing on your vitamin quota,

your hair will show it. Have you ever noticed how limp the hair of sick people becomes? Their lack of vitality is immediately reflected in their hair. And have you noted, too, that as a sick person regains his health, the hair begins to get back its sheen and gloss as well?

Therefore keep constantly in mind the necessity of eating your daily food requirements. Keep up your supply of nutrients and vitamins so that your physical condition is tiptop.

But food alone will not make healthy hair. To be fully healthy, hair must also be clean. Dirty hair not only looks unattractive, it behaves unattractively. It falls in greasy strands and refuses to hold a wave. Furthermore, dirty hair means a dirty scalp, and — — dandruff.

Dandruff is not only a most unpleasant condition to look at; it is also harmful to the hair. It indicates an uncared-for scalp, and one that is not giving the hair roots their proper nourishment. When dandruff scales start to sprinkle your coat collar, it follows that something is amiss with the scalp.

Dandruff can and ought to be corrected. A bad case of dandruff can cause the skin to break out and wreck an otherwise attractive complexion. Dandruff also can ruin a well-coifed head of hair. Think of the torture it must be for the boy danc-

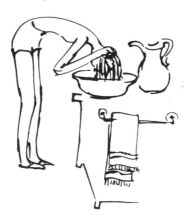

ing with you, who must look down on a part that lays bare a scaling scalp.

To get rid of dandruff, set yourself a routine. Wash your hair often with a shampoo designed to combat dandruff (ask your druggist to recommend a good one) and brush your hair vigorously, being careful to get the bristles well down into the roots.

Brushing is essential for beautiful hair. Not just lackadaisical brushing, but good stiff get-in-there-and-dig brushing. Brushing stimulates the scalp, encourages good circulation of the blood to the hair roots (which makes for well-nourished hair) and picks up loose dirt that dulls the color of the hair. A good brushing job should leave the scalp feeling tingly.

To be adequately brushed, hair should be stroked at least one hundred times each night. A good rule is to brush until your arm gets tired. Put your head down and start with the brush at the roots of the hair and then follow the hair down to the tips with clean firm strokes.

Combing never replaces brushing. Do not think that because you comb your hair frequently you can get away with a few swipes of the hairbrush. Not for a minute. Combing merely puts the hair in place; it does not give glow and gloss to the hair, as a brush does. You should of course comb your hair in order to keep it well groomed. But combing should be thought of as a finishing touch, not as a basic beauty aid.

There are two important rules to remember about combing and brushing. One is just plain good manners, and that is never to comb or brush your hair in a public place. The second rule is designed to promote hair health: never borrow or lend your comb and brush. Dirty utensils can transfer dandruff from one head to another. A broken comb, one with miss-

ing teeth, can cause ends to split. Therefore, in view of these hazards, it is far better to keep your own utensils to yourself and be personally responsible for seeing that they are kept clean and in first-rate condition.

Shampooing your comb and brush is just as important as shampooing your hair. Do both frequently; if anything, shampoo your comb and brush more often than your hair. Dirty combs and brushes applied to clean hair nullify all the good work of a recent shampoo.

When it comes to shampooing your own hair, plan to save at least one night a week for the job. Most teens prefer Thursday night because it puts their hair in shape for the week-end. Some teens may even want to do their hair more often, particularly if it is inclined to be oily. Doing your own hair will save money, so that when you really want a professional beauty parlor job, you will have the cash on hand to pay for it.

In between your beauty parlor trips,

you can keep your hair in shape by brushing and shampooing. Shampoo your hair regularly with a good shampoo, one that agrees with your hair—an oily hair needs a drying shampoo, a dry head of hair needs a castile-type shampoo. Do use a good shampoo; do not use an ordinary cake of bath soap. It is almost impossible to make bath soap dissolve completely into lather, and the chances are that it will not rinse out well. A residue will remain on the hair that will dull its shine and make it sticky to the touch. Well-rinsed hair should squeak.

It is not difficult to do a professional shampoo at home. It merely takes a bit of organization. Before you start, make certain that you have all the necessary equipment: shampoo, hot water and a clean towel.

Begin your shampoo by brushing your hair thoroughly. Then tub your head well in water, apply the shampoo, and scrub. Work up a good lather and make sure that it penetrates every square inch. Now rinse out the first lather and start afresh. With the second lathering you should have removed all the dirt. Then rinse your hair three times. With the third rinsing, you should hear the hair squeak as it runs between your fingers.

Next comes a clean towel, which you should use first to wring out the moisture from your hair and then to massage the scalp—thereby soaking up even more hard-to-get-at moisture still clinging to the hair. If possible, brush your hair dry in the sunlight. If not, at least brush it frequently during the drying process.

After the shampoo comes the setting. Indeed, for some teens setting comes every night of the week, shampoo or no, and for those who learn to do a first-rate job, the rewards will be great. Ultimately, the way your hair looks after it

is taken down from the curling apparatus depends upon how skillfully it has been put up.

Setting hair well does not take professional knowledge, but it does take a little time. However, the more you do it, the more adept you become and the less time the process involves. Some girls can put up their hair (even those with short-cropped hair that involves many, many pin curls) in the time it takes most people to brush their teeth.

There is one general rule that makes hair setting a success, whether your hair be long or short: it is not advisable to set your hair while it is wet. Wet hair that is allowed to dry during the curling process will emerge kinky and sausage-tight. A better method is to set your hair when it is dry and then to wrap your head turban-fashion, with a towel that has been wrung out in very hot water. The steam from the towel will penetrate the rolled-up curls and dampen each slightly. This dampness will be sufficient to give each curl the required amount of moisture to make it set, but not so much that the curl is drowned.

Let the towel turban remain on your head for five minutes. Then remove it, and put a net around your head to hold the curls in place. Allow your hair about fifteen minutes' time to dry out completely. When you unfurl your curls, lo and behold, you will discover that your hair is soft and delicate, not frizzed like a South Sea Islander's. This curl, by the way, will withstand any amount of brushing. Don't be afraid to attack your hair after it has been set. Curl will not come out if it has been properly set and if the hair is truly dry.

While this rule for dry-setting holds for any length of hair, it is true that different lengths of hair do demand slightly different curling techniques. Short hair cannot be set in the same way as long hair. If you change your hair length, then you must also change your setting technique.

If your hair is long (to your shoulders), the best way to set it is with rag curlers. These, unlike metal ones, will not split the ends, and they are lots more comfortable to sleep on. To give the rag, which by its very nature is rather limp, additional firmness, first fold it lengthwise over a twice folded facial tissue. Then place the rag lengthwise across the end of the strand of hair to be curled and roll up the hair in it. Hold it in place by tying the two ends of the rag together. For most teens, two rags at each side and two in the back are sufficient.

If your hair is short, on the other hand, rag curlers will not do the trick. Short hair needs to be curled in very small sections, each section no more than a wisp or two. Roll each wisp over your finger and secure it with a metal clip or hairpin. Make certain that you put in enough pins to hold each curl in position. By putting a hair net over the whole business, you can reduce the chances of a curl slipping out of place.

When you have become really expert at putting up your own hair, you may want to try a home permanent. I would not advise you to try one if you are all thumbs with your tresses, because it is too easy to bungle the job. A home permanent is based on one's ability to handle hair with ease. But many teens with the practice and experience of doing their own hair day after day should have all the skill required.

If you decide to try a home permanent, read all the directions carefully and follow each to the letter. Do not try any short cuts of your own. Best of all, give yourself a home permanent over a weekend, when you have time to take pains.

About the only thing a teen cannot do well by herself is to cut her own hair. Cutting and shaping takes professional know-how. There is a great deal more to it than hacking with scissors or a razor. Unless you have an uncanny knowledge of what you are doing with your hands at the back of your head when you can't see them you had better leave the cutting to a professional.

Basic to any good-looking coiffure is a well cut, well shaped head of hair. It is almost impossible to set hair well if it is unevenly trimmed or too thick and bushy.

With the pennies you save by doing your own shampoos and settings, you can afford to have your hair cut at a beauty parlor. If your hair is short, you need to have it shaped at least once a month. If your hair is long, you can wait longer, but not so long that it gets out of kilter and straggly about the edges.

Now that you have patiently borne with me while I discussed all the things you need to know in order to keep your hair healthy and in good condition, you will want to ask, "But how should I wear my hair?" Unfortunately, that is a question for which I have no general rule. There is no one all-becoming hair style. Every girl needs to wear her hair the way that suits her best. By experiment she usually finds her own best style.

Still there are a few guideposts that beauticians and hair stylists have devised for choosing the most flattering hair style. These guideposts are based on the assumption that the oval face is the most beautiful, and in consequence the hair should be so arranged as to make every face seem to be oval.

Aside from the admired classic oval face, there are five other types of faces. They are:

1. The round.
2. The square.
3. The long and narrow.
4. The heart (wide at forehead, narrow at chin).
5. The pear (narrow at forehead, wide at jaw).

The teen with the round face needs to give an illusion of length. Her hair then should be styled with interest at the top. The sides should be kept smooth and her hair brushed away from her face. The simpler the hair style, the better. Too sweet curls look babyish.

The teen with the square face needs to soften her somewhat severe and angular lines. A short bang or flip at the forehead is a flattering touch. Hair that is short and brushed away from the temples and curled behind the eartips looks well. She should never have her hair cut so that it just comes to the angle of the jaw. Long hair rolled under in a page-boy and kept behind the ears, or short hair smoothed flat at the sides should suit her best.

The teen with the long and narrow face needs to give herself more width. She should always have her hair softly waved, as severely cut straight hair will tend to emphasize her long face. In-between lengths are the best, and a bang over the forehead will shorten the distance between hairline and jaw.

The teen with the heart-shaped face needs to give more width to her jaw. She should try to wear her hair in such a way that fullness fills out her jawline with the hair covering the ears. Again a soft bang at the forehead will help to mask the width.

The teen with the pear-shaped face needs to make more of her forehead, less of her jaw. She can give width on top by giving herself a flip of hair, like half a bang, or dipping the hair gently at one side. She should keep the interest to the top and have her hair at the bottom short enough to curl just slightly over the edges of the jaw, masking some of the width.

The teen with the oval face may do as she pleases. Long, short, or in-between, she can go the way she wants. Because she has so many possibilities, she should try to keep herself in the forefront of fashion, trying out each new hair style as it comes along.

Teens with other than oval faces, however, need not feel that they cannot change with the fashions. Because the rules say add width, or give an illusion of length, there is no reason to stick to them too rigidly. Many girls have flaunted all the rules with great success. However, if you do it, make sure you are doing it for the best.

The most successful time to experiment with your hair is when it is being shampooed. Hair that is stiff with lather can be twisted and turned like molasses taffy. The next time your hair is washed, before you rinse out the lather, spend five minutes in front of your mirror, arranging it in new positions. You might very well discover a much more exciting way to wear your hair. Never be afraid to experiment. If you cut your hair, it can always grow back. If you curl it, you can always uncurl it again. As long as you have hair, you need never feel that anything you do is irredeemable.

Most important of all, don't let yourself become a fuddy-duddy about fashion. Don't stick to a pompadour when it has gone out of style. Don't keep on wearing your hair the same old way, when the passé styles make you look old hat. Don't throw caution to the winds, of course, but do discover that you can stick to the basic hairstyle guideposts and still change your hair when you want to. Remember that a pompadour adds height, but so does a flipped-up bang. In hair, as in anything else, there is always more than one way to skin a cat.

The real secret of lovely hair is sleekness. Hair that is soft, gleaming, shaped, and shining will never go out of date. Fancy bits of business like spit curls and one-inch bobs may come and go, but well-groomed hair will stay forever. If you keep your hair healthy, if you change the style often enough, you can count on it that you will be known as a girl with beautiful hair.

ROUND 1 | 2 SQUARE

LONG 3 | 4 HEART

PEAR 5 | 6 OVAL

5

Makeup

"Nothing I do ever seems to make me look any better."

There is nothing so discouraging as spending a lot of time fussing around with your face and then feeling when you have finished that nothing has been accomplished. I know how grim that feeling can be. It took me some time before I got the knack of making myself up well. In the process of trial and error I discovered this fact: a good deal of the success in makeup comes from first knowing what and then knowing how to make up.

What to make up is the first problem.

Some of us make up too much of our faces. Others don't make up enough. Finding the happy medium is the problem. Even when that happy medium has been established, we still have the problem of how, and that's where most of us fall down. For my part, I think that the answer to the question of how-to lies in the phrase "keep a straight face." That is, put your makeup on neatly and evenly. Don't be satisfied until you have a perfect job. A pretty mouth turned topsy-turvy by a hasty application of lipstick is no credit to anybody's face.

Many of the problems about makeup stem from the fact that nobody ever told you how to go about it. From that blissful day when your mother told you it was all right to wear a little lipstick to that big party until now, you have been going along in a kind of hit-or-miss fashion. Well, this is the time to get down to the basic fundamentals and learn what's what about makeup. It won't take long.

One of the first things to learn is that you must never let your makeup look obvious. First and foremost, makeup should look natural, not artificial. That means that you have to be artful about your artifice—and that's where the little tricks come in. Some of these tricks will seem time-consuming and some too picayune to bother about, but they are all important to the final, happy result. Just wait and see.

Good makeup begins with a good base. Powder base helps make the powder stick and consequently stays on longer. It also acts as a protection to the skin in weather and at the same time helps cover over flaws. One thing I want to get straight at this point is that powder base is not pancake. A good base is a cream or lotion that lets the pores breathe. The trouble with pancake is that it blocks up the pores and can cause eruptions. Also, unless very skillfully used, pancake looks too much like a mask. From my point of view, one of the best powder bases is a mild hand lotion. Apply it to your face just as you would to your hands.

On top of the powder base goes the powder. One of the most important points here is the color you choose. Powder should match the color of your skin; it should be neither darker nor lighter. One of the best investments you can make is to have your powder individually blended to your skin tone. Thus, as your skin color changes, as it becomes tanned in summer or paler in winter, the color of your powder can change with it.

If you do not have your powder blended, then be careful to choose carefully from the numerous kinds available. Get as close a match to your skin as possible. Do not make the mistake of thinking that a pale pinky powder over an olive skin will make you seem all peaches and cream or that a dark powder over a fair skin will make you look tanned. You won't get the effect. What you will get is the rather untidy result of wearing a sheer white organdy dress over a black slip or vice versa. Don't forget that your skin color is your own—part of nature's

individual plan for you—so take it the way you find it and make the most of it.

The powder of your selection should be applied with a clean puff—a new one every day. To make sure that you have a constant supply on hand, buy those inexpensive little packages that contain a dozen or so of the small puffs designed specifically to be discarded after one use. In a pinch, clean cotton will do the trick, but if you use it be careful to remove any fuzz it may leave on the skin.

Puff your powder on, oh, so sparingly, and then brush off the excess. Never have your powder look as though you dunked your head in the box. If possible, work under a strong light so that you can see what you are doing. That way you will make certain to powder well up into the hairline and down into the area of the neck and ears. Don't leave any high-water marks.

The purpose of powder is to give the skin a smooth, even surface, to dull shine and to disguise rough bumps. Powder well applied will make your complexion seem luminous. Essentially, powder does not put color in your cheeks. That is the function of rouge. However, few teenagers need to add color, for their skins have a glowing light of their own derived from an active outdoor life.

I personally don't advise rouge for teens, but if there are some who feel that they are utterly washed out without it, then a very little bit high on the cheekbone and with the outlines blended well is permissible. But for Heaven's sake, use only a little. Rouge goes a long way. Proms and parties, where you will be looked at under artificial light, are the best occasions to try out rouge (if you must), for the strong unnatural lighting will soften the coloring.

Lipstick is a horse of a different color. With lipstick you can be lavish. Clear reds and strong pinks are good colors to work with. Pale anemic shades and raucous purples and fuchsias are better left alone. Pale pinks tend to make the mouth look bloodless, and strong purples look too much like blood. In the ranges of the true reds lie the happiest choices. There is a wide selection of colors from orange reds to cherry reds, and among them teens should find enough to meet all their requirements.

When it comes to applying lipstick, use a brush. A brush will more accurately define the lip edges, and once you get the hang of it, it is easier to wield than the

blunt end of a lipstick. Use the brush to draw the outlines of your mouth and the blunt stick to fill in the rest.

Now, you ask, what outline should I draw? Generally speaking, one should follow the natural curves of the mouth, but some improvements can be made on nature. Most mouths can be divided into the four following classifications:

1. The wide, full.
2. The small bow.
3. The long, thin.
4. The full under or upper lip.

Starting with any one of these outlines, a girl can make her mouth over to a more becoming shape. The girl with a wide, full mouth should use her brush to draw an outline somewhat smaller than the natural outline. The girl with a small bow (since the small bow went out of fashion with Clara Bow, who was a famous beauty before your time) should enlarge the natural outline, particularly as she goes toward the tapering points. The girl with the long, thin mouth should increase the width of her mouth at the center, and the girl with a full under (or upper) lip should decrease the size of the larger lip and increase the smaller one to bring both into balance.

All this, my friends, is possible with a lip brush.

One further point about applying lipstick that many teens (and many adults) don't realize is that lipstick should not be used in the very corners of the mouth. If so used, it will smear. Instead draw your outline not quite to the corner and then stop. Another trick to prevent smearing or caking is to dust your lips with powder before putting on lipstick and then, after applying it, blot your mouth well with tissue.

Even if you learn to make your mouth the most enticing one possible, it will profit you little unless you take care of your teeth. A well made-up mouth should be a frame for your teeth; it should call attention to their whiteness and their gleam. To keep your teeth white and gleaming, brush them at least twice every day. The best time to brush is before and after meals, which would mean, if you discount lunch, four times a day. This may seem like a lot of times, but the results are worth it. If you don't feel that you can stick to such a conscientious schedule, try to remember to give your teeth a good brushing once every morning and once every night. At the same time, rinse your mouth with a good mouthwash. This practice will keep your mouth fresh and clean, destroy particles of food that may cause cavities, and make your breath sweet and pleasant.

A trip to the dentist twice a year is a must. The dentist, as a specialist, will be able to take care of any problems that may pop up from time to time and so prevent you from having serious difficulties. By postponing your visit you gain nothing but the possibility of a very large toothache. A beautiful smile is a necessary attribute to beauty, so if you want to look like a cover girl you've got to look after your teeth.

Eyes, like teeth, have to last you a lifetime, so take good care of them. If you need glasses, wear glasses. The old prejudice about girls with glasses being unattractive has long since passed away. Nowadays glasses are so nicely designed—in a variety of shapes with frames of various colors—that I know of girls who don't wear them envying girls who do.

As to making up your eyes, don't. Young eyes need no enhancement. They have their own sparkle and flashes of fire, so why bury them under gobs of goo? Mascara and eyebrow pencil, like rouge, are artifices best left to others. Teenagers who come to school with colored blobs above each eyelid look plain silly.

If you are going somewhere extra special, a big prom perhaps, and you feel that you just have to look glamorous, then try a little Vaseline or cream on each eyelid. Just this little touch will bring out all you need to give your eyes a triumphant twinkle. But no goo. And for that special prom, all your eyebrows need is a bit of combing to make them lie flat. The few stray hairs that fall out of line may be tweezed out with a tweezer. Just the few stray hairs, though, not the whole eyebrow.

To review, then, what any teen-ager needs to keep a straight face, we find that the following are all that is really necessary: powder base, powder, lipstick, and for evening a bit of rouge and a bit of Vaseline or cream. These simple ingredients, used with skill, will do the work and do it well. Above all, remember that each and every one of these ingredients must be removed from the face every day. Every time you make up afresh you should start with a clean face. New makeup should never go on top of old. It not only looks stiff and cakey, but it also seals up pores and encourages blackheads and skin eruptions.

Just as no teen-ager is ever stuck with the face she was born with, in view of the ways she has to make up her features to their best advantage, so no teen is ever stuck with the hands she was born with. Well-cared-for hands, be they long and thin, short and broad, or in-between, can be beautiful.

The first requisite for pretty hands is that they be kept soft and smooth. Use hand lotion at least once a day. Better still, use hand lotion every time you wash your hands, to replace the oils that the soap and water have removed. If your hands are particularly rough and chapped, carry a small bottle of lotion around with you to use at odd moments during the day.

A weekly manicure performed every Thursday night when you shampoo your hair, will, if well done, be sufficient. Weekly care of the hands is important because neatly trimmed nails, gently tapered, can go a long way toward making a hand look attractive. Nails are the focal point of the hand, so give them your attention.

To keep your nails strong and flexible so that they can be filed into becoming shape with all ten of them more or less equal in length—not nine talons and one stub—be sure to eat leafy green vegetables and drink lots of milk. Nails, like hair, are alive. They are not dead structures that have been tacked on to your body as an afterthought. Keep them healthy with proper diet and proper care.

The Thursday night routine—I choose Thursday night because that is generally the night you choose to wash your hair—should encompass all the necessities of good hand care. First wash your hands to get them clean; if they are really grimy, use a brush to get out every bit of dirt. Make certain to get at the dirt beneath the nails, too.

Next, file your nails. Trim away rough edges. Use an emery board for this, since a metal file is too harsh and tends to split the nail ends. Don't file too deeply at the corners. Nails should be rounded curves; they should not describe a gothic arch.

When your nails are filed to satisfaction, take a cuticle stick and cuticle remover and gently push back the cuticle. Do not cut it. Cuticle will respond to treatment, and if weekly care is given it will not overstep its bounds.

When your nails are filed and the cuticle softened, you are ready to put on the nail base, a clear lacquer that prepares the way for the polish. Cover the whole nail with the base and let it dry thoroughly before you start the polish.

After the base has dried, the next step is to apply the first coat of polish. Cover the whole nail; it is easier than trying to describe an accurate curve around the moon. When the first coat dries, apply the second. To make the polish last, cover a fingertip of the free hand with a bit of tissue and remove the very edge of polish from the nail. In this way the polish will not be chipped by constant contact with hard surfaces. On top of the last (second) coat of polish goes the top coat, a clear lacquer like the base, which protects the polish.

The secret of a good manicure is the careful following out of each of these procedures. Most important of all is to let each coat dry. Do not use your hand until you are certain that each nail is dry; otherwise the still sticky polish will pick up the imprints of the things you touch. Nail polish, if applied this way, should last out the week. If one finger does chip, you can do an emergency touch-up. But if more than one fingernail chips, start the whole process from the beginning. Nothing looks more patched up than touched-over nails.

In choosing your polish colors, keep in mind the lipsticks you use most often. Polish and lipstick need not match but they should harmonize. Pink polish with tangerine lipstick is an out-and-out horror. As with lipstick, choose polish colors from the real reds and lively pinks; leave to others the passionate purples.

Remember that it is daily care as well as weekly care that keeps your hands in condition. Keep your hands clean every day. Always have an emery board handy to file down rough snags and nail scissors to cut away a hangnail before you get impatient and pull and bite at it.

A hint for hand care that I can recommend is the use of a pumice to smooth down calluses. Many teens are bothered with a bump on their middle finger, which is caused by the pressure of a pencil. This school girl's badge can be rubbed down with a pumice when your hands are wet. With attention to little details such as these, you can have hands you will be proud of, so that when you want to show off your class ring or, better still, *his* class ring, you can do it with pride.

Feet as well as hands deserve care. In the summer especially they need some sort of attention for they are very much in view. Cut your toenails straight across and keep them short. Long nails cause stocking runs. If you wish, polish your toenails, matching the color to your hands. A bit

of baby oil used daily at the back of your heel will prevent roughness caused by constant rubbing against your shoe.

And from head to toe, that's all there is to makeup. It is really very easy; all that is required is know-how, which comes with practice. If you don't succeed the first time, try again and again.

6

Modeling
Tricks

"See that model. Gee, I wish I looked like that."

Did you ever watch a magician pull a rabbit out of a hat or make a dollar bill disappear? If you have, you've marveled how he ever managed to do it. Then, later, when someone explained to you how the trick was done, you ceased to marvel; the mystery became commonplace. The very same thing applies to models. When you come to understand the aces that a model holds up her sleeve, you cease to wonder why she is so beautiful

and begin to see how you too can be a beauty.

There are tricks in modeling, just as there are tricks in magic-making. In fact, there is a great deal of similarity between magicians and models, because both have a wonderful degree of control over their muscles. It is the magician's muscle control that enables him to make a coin disappear, and it is a model's control of her muscles that makes her look so straight and tall.

You never see a model slouch, you

never see a model with her fanny poked out or her chin resting on her breastbone. A model knows that good posture is basic to a good figure, and that a good carriage goes hand in hand with a good posture. Not even the most perfect figure from the point of view of the tape measure can look well if it is slumped in the midsection and thrust out of joint at the hip.

To look your best you must get in the habit of standing tall—all in one line. Pull up from the top of your head. Tuck your fanny under and get your hips in line. Keep your chest high and your tummy in. Someone once told me to stand as if I wore a beautiful jewel that I wanted to show off at my bosom, and I think perhaps it is the best advice I can pass on to you.

One of the worst faults most of us have is that we do not stand up. Even when we are in a vertical position in relation to the ground, we still tend to sit down. Our rib cages are slumped into our waistline and our shoulders are bent forward. One way to correct this habit is to concentrate on your rib cage.

Think about it and try consciously to pull it up out of your waistline. A deep breath will show you how much you can bring your whole chest area up into the air. Even if you could, you wouldn't have to hold your breath all the time in order to achieve good posture, but a deep breath every now and then is a good idea. It will help pull you into line.

Many teens seem to walk head first into everything—that is to say, they lead with their chin. This aggressive attitude comes from standing with the head jutted forward, shoulders slumped, and eyes focused on the ground. To correct this, bring your shoulders back, hold your neck straight, and let your chin fall into place so that it is directly above your breast-

Not like this.

But like this.

bone. Keep your eyes straight ahead; you don't have to look after your feet, they'll take care of themselves. It won't hurt a bit if, in the beginning, you carry this position to West Point extremes until you get the feel of what it is really like to stand tall.

How you stand greatly influences how you walk. It may seem like a little thing, but an ungainly walk can be the ruin of even the most attractive girl. You'll realize this when you think how often comedians use a person's walk to characterize humor. Mimics who mock shuffling gaits, knock-kneed and pigeon-toed walks, are funny on the stage, but if you walk that way in real life you'll come to grief. Look to your own walk and see how it would bear up under criticism.

Furthermore, if only because clothes look well on girls who stand and walk well, you will want to practice good walking. A model works on her walk constantly, because she knows that to show off a design to its best advantage she has to move her body gracefully.

This is the way a model walks. Her feet are pointed straight ahead—toes neither in nor out. She moves her leg from the hip in a swinging stride and puts her heel down first. Every time she takes a step she picks up her feet; she does not just push them along. She holds her weight high and puts her feet down lightly, not as if they were bearing the full load of her body.

To walk gracefully one must move the leg in one piece. The movement should start at the point where the leg is joined to the hip and continue in an unbroken line to the ankle. In that way the leg moves forward in one sweeping movement, instead of propelling itself by a series of awkward disjointed jerks. These jerks you sometimes see come from bending the knee as you walk and actually using the movement as the point from which the forward movement begins. Get in the habit of moving your leg from the hip—if you've ever studied modern dance, you'll know the feeling it gives, the sensation of fluid movement.

Some of you may have found this insistence of mine on how you stand and walk rather silly and tedious. I hope you won't think so when I point out to you that your posture and carriage greatly bear on how well you dance. A girl who stands with a sway back all day long is not magically going to change and be erect on the dance floor. Oh, no; her fanny will be just as outstanding—and what's more, it may be even worse, since her back is bent slightly more than normal as she leans against her partner. A girl who shuffles her feet along school corridors and city pavements will still shuffle every bit as much on the dance floor; moreover, she'll probably shuffle right onto the long suffering toes of her partner. To be light on your feet, you have to pick your feet up and put them down again in a definite, precise movement.

Give some thought to how you look when you are dancing. After all, what the stag line sees of you is your posture—your face is hidden in the crook of your partner's arm. It is your back that is on display —plus the way you hold yourself. If you're sagging in the middle and dispiritedly moving along, you won't be a pretty sight from the sidelines. So the next time you get up to dance, pull in those tummy muscles, tuck in your fanny, pull up your rib cage, and then dance. If you keep your arm lightly on your partner's shoulder and your head high, you'll look as light as a thistledown, be you five feet one or five feet eleven.

Right now is as good a time as any to banish a misconception that many tall girls have. They believe that they· can camouflage their height by slumping. Well, it is just not true. If you are tall,

you'll still look tall if you slump, and you'll be awkward besides. There is nothing to be done about height except to wear it well. Stand up to your full number of inches and be proud that you can see over the crowd. Tall girls are blessed with their height, for they and they alone can wear the extremes of fashion. Most models are tall; they have to be in order to show off complicated clothes.

If most of the boys you know are unfortunately shorter than you, you won't get down to their level by slumping, so what's the use trying and ruining your appearance in the process? Chances are that in time you'll find a man as tall as you, and in the meantime make the best of it. Be consoled by the fact that the long-legged gal is the gal most often selected as the typical American beauty.

More than medium-sized girls and short ones, tall girls understand the importance of shoes. They know the difference it makes to wear a pair of flats or a pair of heels. In the main, it is better for everyone, short or tall, to wear flats during the day. They give your feet the proper support and good balance. Good balance is a necessary part of graceful movement—as you realized, perhaps, the first time you tried on ice skates and found that your balance depended on two thin blades.

In choosing your flats don't get too low down. Do be careful to select those with a little heel. Absolutely flat shoes do not give the foot sufficient support, with the result that your heel tends to turn inward and your whole foot is thrown out of line. Ballet slippers were designed for ballerinas to dance in, not to walk in.

At the opposite end of the scale, when buying your party slippers don't go to the other extreme and buy the spindliest heel you can find. Very few people can balance on such precarious pinpoints. Keep your heel height a happy medium, about half-inch heels for flats and anywhere from two to two and a half for good pumps.

If you are unaccustomed to wearing a heel, even the most moderate kind, try out your new heels before appearing at a party. Nothing looks quite so ridiculous as a girl mincing about in a pair of heels which she has not yet learned how to handle. Remember that your balance changes with your heel height, so be sure you know how to make the adjustment before you soar out on your next date.

One of the most important things for any teen to realize is that she is always on display—except in the privacy of her own bedroom. That is why you should practice your posture, your walk, and even how to handle your heels. You are being looked at by somebody every time you walk down the street, twirl on the dance floor, or drink a Coke at the drugstore. Therefore, keep your muscles in trim and your body in line so that you need never fear how you look.

A model learns by practice how to keep herself in line. She is not afraid to catch a glimpse of herself in a store mirror, because she knows that she is standing tall and walking freely. You can tell from the way she moves that she knows what she is about. A model has reached the point where she has so disciplined her muscles

that they behave the way they ought to without having to be constantly reminded.

If you've ever watched a model in repose, you'll notice that she stands with one foot at a right angle to the other, rather like a ballet dancer. She takes this pose so often before the camera that it becomes natural to her. It would be well if it became natural to you, for it is one of the most flattering and comfortable ways to stand.

The reason that this particular pose has been selected out of all others is that it throws the body into profile. The camera, you know, adds ten pounds to a figure, and therefore the less body you show to it, the less it has to work with. Thus a trained model knows how to stand three-quarter view, hips in profile and shoulders swung forward.

These are good hints to bear in mind when you are having your picture taken. If you remember just a few of them you'll never have reason to regret a snapshot. The awful part of snapshots usually is

that the ones we like least turn out to be the ones people save, so, if you're guided by these suggestions, you'll reduce your chances of having unflattering pictures of you in public view.

One of the cardinal rules of posing for a picture is to remember that whatever is nearest the camera will photograph the largest. If you are snapped on the beach with your legs and feet pointing straight on, your big toe will look as large as your head. If you put out your hand toward the camera, like a policeman directing traffic, your hand will seem as large as your torso.

Of all the parts of the body, hands are usually the hardest to control when posing for a picture. Often the best thing to do with them is to lose them—that is, put them behind your back or in some way get them out of the picture. You can put them at your waist with your elbows akimbo if you choose. It takes a great deal of skill to manage hands well—actresses are often noted for the way they use their hands—but ordinary human beings seem

to get tangled in them, with too many fluttery gestures. So unless you know what to do with your hands, the best thing to do is nothing.

Next to hands, legs are most difficult to tuck away neatly. Especially in beach snapshots, they seem to extend from the body in alarming proportions. If you are having a picture taken at the beach, get your legs in profile with your knees slightly bent. If you want your face turned toward the camera, keep your legs to the side, but turn your shoulders full on. This will give a full view of your face, but keep your legs in proportion. Lying, standing or sitting, always try to keep your legs together, not sprawled apart.

Thinking about all these things at once before the camera goes click is not easy to do. A model learns how to do it fast because she has to do it often. But any girl can learn to do it too with a little practice. It is a valuable lesson in muscle control. If you doubt it, just try holding any pose you fancy for a half a minute—not so easy as it sounds, is it?

Learning how to make your body move the way you want it to and make it stay that way is good training for coordination. And muscular coordination is something that will stand you in good stead all your life. Coordination counts—in the field of sports, on the dance floor, and even in the business of having your picture taken.

One of the most-looked-at pictures any teen has taken is the picture for her school yearbook. This picture need not ever cause any qualms if you give some thought to it. Remember all the little things I have been pointing out in this chapter and you'll make a pretty finished print.

Keep in mind that an absolutely flat full-face view is not flattering. Slightly three-quarters to full profile will do more for your features. Your photographer will be aware of all this, of course, and pose you accordingly. So do what he says without quibbling.

To a photography appointment wear a white tailored blouse (unless your school has a prescribed uniform). Wear no jewelry, except perhaps a strand of pearls. As to makeup, wear lipstick and a bit of powder—take your photographer's advice as to how much to put on. Above all, do not change your hair style before your appointment—such experiments may turn out too disastrously, and you don't want to go down in history looking like a freak. Do go to your appointment with your hair arranged neatly, clean, and well combed.

7

Good Grooming

"If only she weren't so sloppy."

This remark uttered ruefully or indignantly has caused the downfall of many an attractive teen-ager. Girls whisper about it behind her back. Boys mutter about it in their locker rooms. The word gets around and dates come few and far between. And the pity of it is that such unpleasant ostracism is easily preventable. No girl need be pushed out of the social swim simply because she is too lazy to look after herself.

It's no joke that you can't be too careful about your personal habits. When it comes right down to the facts of the case, nothing can beat day-to-day attention to details. As a model, I realize how true this is. Nobody wants to book a girl with dirty fingernails or a torn blouse. And certainly nobody wants to work with a model who stints on bathing and doesn't use a deodorant.

When you were a child it was all very well to skip your daily bath. It was a cute trick. But now that you are in your teens, such actions are no longer cute. They're tiresome. A dirty child will be excused, a dirty teen-ager never. Even if she is wearing the most expensive clothes, no teen can look alluring if her hair is badly combed, her nails grimy, her blouse spotted and her body generally un-washed.

A daily bath or shower should be the minimum for everyone. When you are planning to go out on a date, a second tub or shower should be taken. In the summer two baths a day are not excessive. Remember, too, that the tub is not a thing to hop in and out of. Plan instead to spend some time there once you're in. Soap thoroughly and really get the dirt off. Be sure also to remove all the soap and to dry yourself throroughly from head to toe —and between the toes.

After every bath you should use a good deodorant. There is no time of year when this precaution should be omitted. In summer the heat makes it essential, as everybody perspires freely. The rest of the year the body gives off enough perspira-tion-to justify a deodorant, particularly in winter, when hot houses and woolen clothing join forces. Remember, too, that woolens and sweaters should be cleaned often to remove any odor that may cling stubbornly to them.

If you perspire from nervousness, as many do, don't be alarmed, it is just a normal bodily reaction. However, if you know that you are subject to this sort of thing, be scrupulously careful. If you feel the necessity sew protective shields in your blouses and dresses. No one should ever slip up on these simple procedures. An ounce of prevention is worth a pound of cure. A date once made uncomfortable or a friend offended by your carelessness will take a long time to forget.

In addition to deodorants, you should get in the habit of using a light scent—any flower cologne will do, provided that it is fresh and fragrant. Dab a little behind

each ear and at your neckline and along the length of each arm. There is no need to fear a liberal use of it, since cologne is not perfume. Its fragrance is light and passing. Before a date, it is an especially nice touch to sprinkle your hair with a drop or two.

I can't think of a nicer compliment than that of being told, "How nice you smell." To achieve this distinction, it is necessary to get accustomed to the use of cologne and to a cologne that is right for you. Which is the right one, I cannot say. A little experimentation will decide that for you—cologne is an individual matter and you should choose one that fits you. But do experiment and do pick one out and use it in preference to a perfume which is too highly concentrated an es-sence to be used effectively when you are young. Perfume, if incorrectly used, has a heavy, oversweet odor, but cologne is always refreshing, always pleasant.

Next to a deodorant, daily use of a re-liable mouthwash is important. I have spoken before of the importance of taking care of your teeth and I only want to emphasize the business of rinsing and gargling. This is such a little thing and so easy to do that it will forestall the possibil-ity of bad breath. If you are meticulous in this habit, at no time need you fear that you are offending.

The necessity of using deodorants and

mouth rinses is hardly disputable. They are as expected a part of daily routine as wearing shoes on the street. But when it comes to the question of to shave or not to shave, many teens find themselves in the toils of conflicting theories. Some think they should, others think they shouldn't. Some are afraid that if they do, the hairs will grow in blacker and bushier.

From the point of view of good grooming, I feel that one should shave. Even if your hair is very blond, I still am convinced that legs and underarms are sleeker and more dainty if they are clean-shaven. Furthermore, it is not true that shaving will cause the hair to grow back thicker or any darker in color. It may appear to do so, but that is only because the stubbly ends are more bristly to the touch than the fuller-grown hairs are.

If you decide on shaving, you must then determine to keep it up. You should shave your legs at least once a week and your underarms less often, though in the summer you should be careful to keep after them when you are wearing sleeveless dresses and bathing suits. In the summer also, you may want to shave the whole length of your leg if your hair is exceptionally dark. Otherwise you can shave just to the knee and bleach the rest.

You will never hurt yourself when shaving if you follow these simple precautions. Before you take up a razor, always lather your skin well. Make sure that all the hair is damp and well softened. Then take the razor and shave against the grain, which means from ankle up, holding the razor firmly and pressing gently against the skin. Go slow on curves, take it easy at the anklebone and shinbone, where the skin is close to the bone. You will come out unscathed if you take time, but should you cut yourself, a bit of tissue applied to the nick will take care of the bleeding. When you finish shaving, apply hand lotion to the skin to soften it and prevent chapping and the roughening effects of exposure.

These few paragraphs sum up the basic requirements for personal daintiness. Cleanliness and clean-shavenness will go a long way toward making you an attractive teen-ager, but they won't go the whole way. Coupled with a clean body must be clean clothes. I can not overemphasize how necessary it is to be neat about what

you wear. In fairy tales, Prince Charming may have discerned Cinderella's beauty under the soot and ashes, but the chances are against a modern young man poking through layers of dirt to find his own true love.

Tidiness in dress starts with the very first things you put on. Your underwear should be fresh and neat. You should change it daily and have enough in supply to take care of emergencies. With nylon it is easy to keep your things up-to-date, because it dries so quickly. Even without nylon, you can still keep ahead of the game if you wash each night the things you wore during the day.

As to what to wear under what you wear over, I am firmly of the opinion that almost every teen needs a girdle—not a whaleboned ironclad trap, but some sort of lightweight affair to control the curves. Depending on your girth, you can range all the way from an elasticized panty girdle to a well constructed two-way-stretch job with a fabric panel for extra support.

Don't turn up your nose at the idea of wearing these modern aids to figure beauty. Today's girdle is a far cry from the cantankerous corset Grandmother wore. Nowadays a girdle is so light you scarcely know you have it on, and designers of these garments have whipped up cute little tricks that especially adapt them for young figures.

The reason I am so adamant about girdles is that I know of no other way to keep a figure well in hand. Even a teen with a trim figure needs to coax her curves a bit when it comes to wearing slim skirts and slacks. To me there is nothing more repellent than a protruding fanny or a bulging tummy marring the outline of a narrow silhouette.

So buy a girdle and try a girdle. You'll like the effect. And remember this bit of advice: buy a girdle that fits you. There are many kinds available, all designed to do different jobs. To decide on the one that is best for you takes time. Ask the salespeople in your favorite store to give you some help. Don't be shy about it; that's why they are there.

Good fit is essential in a girdle. And no one girdle fits all teen-age types. There are those who need high waistband models to control midriff tires. There are those

NO
GIRDLE   TOO SMALL
GIRDLE   RIGHT
GIRDLE

who need models with thigh control, those who need the support in the rear, and those who need it in front. So buy what you need and buy it in the right size. A too-tight girdle will only make you bulge all the more, and a too-loose one accomplishes nothing. A good rule to follow is to buy by your waist measurement, but if your hips are larger than your waistline by more than ten inches, then use your hip measurement as the guide.

Just as I advise teens to wear girdles, so do I advise teens to wear bras. Your own bust development will determine what you should select. Here, as in girdles, your figure dictates what kind of bra you need. You may require only a simple bandeau, or you may need the added support of a firm underband with well-shaped cups. Whatever you need, find one that fits and then wear it. Remember also that in summer (and for party formals) you will probably need a strapless job, so don't overlook that department.

Bras and girdles come under the heading of underwear and should be laundered as often as you wear them. Girdles need special care; they should be washed only in lukewarm water, well rinsed, and dried in a towel. Do not wring them dry.

Hang them to dry just as you would anything else, but select a light and airy place.

Stockings are not precisely underwear. They are actually outer wear, but they demand the daily attention lavished on all lingerie in general. Rinse out new stockings before wearing. It helps strengthen threads. Always wash your stockings after each wearing. Use lukewarm water and mild soap flakes. Be careful not to snag them with rough or broken fingernails while pulling them on or off. Given good care, stockings, even the sheerest, should wear a long time.

Stockings and girdles go hand in hand because from one hangs the other. In hitching up your stockings to your garters, be careful to get your seams straight. Take care to fasten the garters at the reinforced top of the stocking, not in the sheer part beneath. Stockings should fit properly so that they don't twist about the leg and so that the reinforced top naturally meets the garter. To look sleek and slim, stockings should fit your leg like a second skin, and they will do so if you take care when you shop to select the size you wear, not the one you guess you wear.

Good fit is important in everything you

wear. You probably think about it only in relation to your outer wear, but it is equally essential in your underwear. A baggy slip will bungle the lines of a sleek dress or skirt. A too-long slip hitched up at the waist will make you seem thick—but even that is preferable to a slip that hangs below the hem of your skirt.

In looking for good fit in slips make sure that you have adequate room for movement without so much room that they seem ready to fall off. A slip should slide on smoothly, should not pull at the shoulders or hang lopsided at the hem. It may seem like a small point, but remember also that color is important. All white is a good basic, but you should have a few dark ones to use with dark sheer dresses. Try to choose your slips as carefully as you do your accessories that show. If you do, you'll never slip up.

When it comes to honest-to-goodness accessories that show—hats, shoes, bags, gloves and scarves—remember to keep them clean and well pressed. Shoes should never get run down at the heel. All leather goods need to be polished—a little elbow grease and some wax will work wonders and make the leather last longer too. White scarves, gloves, and collars—basic standbys—should always look fresh and sparkling clean. Be on the lookout for any torn seams, rips or jagged holes and repair them at once.

All good grooming means attention to details. It is the sum total of all the little things—the neat glove, the sewed-on button, the clean blouse, the freshly pressed skirt, the straight seam, the trim figure. It means looking after yourself and your clothes. It means hanging up your things when you take them off— a skirt that has lain rumpled on the closet floor all night is not going to look like a million dollars the next morning. It means using a clothes brush to remove dust and lint, and it means taking time to remove a stain with a cloth and some spot remover.

Most of all, good grooming means looking well put together. The girl who looks helter-skelter, whose colors don't match, and whose clothes are all awry is not well groomed, nor is the girl who is all pinned together, a perambulating pincushion, bristling like a porcupine at every seam. Pins are all right in their place, in an emergency, but they should be supplanted with something more permanent as soon as possible. You'll never get to be a pin-up girl if you depend on pins to keep you in your clothes.

Here is a morning check-up that you should try before you start for school.

1. Underwear—Is it clean? Does it fit?
2. Blouse or sweater—Is it clean? Does it smell fresh?
3. Skirt—any wrinkles, any spots or stray dirt?
4. Shoes—Are they polished and are they trim at the heels?
5. Stockings or socks—Are they clean? Is the seam straight?
6. A last look, to straighten out a lock of hair, check on nose, chin, and lipstick, and you're off.

8

Clothes

"Gosh, I wish I had her clothes."

How often we envy others their clothes. We think that if we could have the same clothes, if we could afford as many, we too could look as pretty. But, truth to tell, even if a fairy godmother waved a wand and said, "So be it," chances are that what looked well on one girl would look not-so-well on the other. Individual figures present individual problems, and what is sauce for the goose ain't so for the gander.

Whether one goes by hackneyed adages or not, the matter of clothes boils down to the simple principle that one must dress to flatter oneself. Height, weight, general build, color of hair, eyes, and personality all play a part in what kind of clothes to choose.

In spite of these individual considerations, there are a few general rules to guide one. These rules stem from the fact that the eye can be fooled. By optical illusion one can make a tall girl seem shorter, a short one taller, a thin one plumper, and a plump one thinner. All this can be done by a happy arrangement of lines.

Lines are what make up the overall shape of the dress. There are wraparound lines, slim lines, pleated lines, gored lines, diagonal lines, radiating lines. Sometimes the lines are made more obvious by use of patterned fabric, such as plaids and stripes; and sometimes attention is called to lines by appliqué—such as a panel of contrasting color down the front opening of a dress.

By recognizing that such lines exist in every dress, you can then choose those dresses which have lines to flatter you. If you are tall, you want to select styles that tend to cut you down. Horizontal lines are your best bet. If you are short, then look for vertical or up-and-down lines. If you are thin, try for horizontal lines (provided you are also tall) and radiating lines—the effect gained from sunburst tucking and shirring. If you are plump, you want lines that call attention to the upper part of the figure; lines that lead the eye away from hips and waistline—big collars are one answer.

With a judicious study of line goes an equally careful study of color. What colors you choose to wear can have a telling effect on how you look. To find out which colors become you, start by placing yourself in one of the following categories:

1. Brunette—fair skinned.
2. Brunette—dark skinned.
3. Blonde—fair skinned.
4. Blonde—dark skinned.
5. Medium brown—fair to dark skin.
6. Redhead—fair to dark skin.

Note that your skin color is just as important as your hair color in determining what to wear. Too often, teens tend to overlook their skin color and think of themselves only by their hair color.

Brunettes with fair skin should play up the exquisite contrast of light and dark. They can look feminine in pastels, pale pink and blue, in dark shades like navy and deep green; and they can look ravishing in bright green and red.

Brunettes with dark skins can play exotic in tangerine tones, in reds, and in bright greens. They should be careful of yellows that tend to give their skin a sallow cast, but they can look to blues and beiges with success.

Blondes with fair skins need to accent their blondness. If they wear dark colors they should lighten them with a pastel contrast. Navy is wonderful, particularly if freshened with a touch of white, pale pink or pale blue. All the pastels are wonderful to underscore the feminine and willowy look of a blonde. Mauve is a heady choice. As for gray—a good neutral.

Blondes with dark skins need to be careful of yellowing their skins. Keep clear of saffron colors and too-dead neutrals. Freshen up grays and beiges with touches of color at the neckline. Greens and the range of blues are excellent for those with hazel eyes.

Girls with medium brown hair—by far the most numerous, and the predominant American type, should be wary of overdoing the drab lines. Spike neutral grays and beiges with color—a lively, perky color like red, green, or blue. Don't be afraid of color—your medium coloring will react well to color in dress. Yellow in the bright ranges, green in all its variations, and blues, from pale to dark, are very good. True dashing red can be used to good effect.

Redheads should make the most of their coloring. Real redheads are few and far between, and those blessed with such distinctive coloring should make the most of it. Most redheads miss a good bet by timidity. Pink, a color they usually avoid, can be sensational. Red, however, can usually not be worn, as it will clash with the hair color. Blues and greens in all their variations, are naturals for redheads, and white may be most effective, but only if the skin color is clear and alive. A redhead with a dead-white complexion should wear white with caution.

As with all rules, these are made to be broken, but break them only after due consideration. Make sure that every color you choose does something for you, and don't forget that your hair may not change color, but your skin can. It tans in the summer, fades in the winter. Keep that in mind when you buy your new clothes.

Finally, and I would say above all, above consideration of your figure and your color type, remember your personality. Often your personality and your figure type go hand in hand, but if they don't, stick to your personality as the best guide.

If you are the tailored type, if you like to be uncluttered and trim, then choose tailored clothes, simple skirts, classic jackets, box coats. Keep to the simple even in your date dresses—dirndl skirts and shirtwaist blouses or bateau-necked sweaters and jerseys. Use rich fabrics for distinction, make them dominate the silhouette.

If you are all feminine, then choose clothes that play up that quality. Full skirts, jackets fitted and peplum-flared, puffed sleeves, ruffled shoulders and hemlines, delicate touches of ribbon and lace. But in the midst of all these fripperies maintain a sense of balance. Don't overdo. Don't mix peplum and ruffles, lace and bows. Keep feminine but don't dress like a candy box.

If you are in between, go your own sweet way, being feminine one day, tailored the next. But do take some stand —don't overdo the inbetweenness. Get to be known for your sense of color or your sense of accessory. Be the girl who knows her way with a scarf or can do a million and one tricks with a strand of pearls. Develop an outstanding characteristic of dress that people associate with you and you alone.

All of you, feminine, tailored, or in between, have one big desire in common. Teens seems to have a universal aching for that first black dress. Usually this involves a long-drawn-out battle with the family and ends in general weariness and a sense of defeat on both sides. If your family do not want you to choose black because they feel you are too young, don't argue. Navy blue is just as good. Black is a color you'll see a good deal of when you are older, so don't rush headlong into it. It's not worth the fight.

None of this advice is startling or particularly new, but it is sound. Happy mediums have been held up as the happy way of life since philosophy began, and the reason that each new generation comes to rediscover the principle is that, by golly, it works.

Next to knowing your type, and dressing to suit it, you must also be sure of your size. Ill-fitting clothes never look well, and buying clothes that don't fit with the intention of having an extensive alteration job done is an expensive luxury. You will find your clothes fit better if you shop for things you know are in your size range. Most teen-agers fall into three classifications: teen sizes for the younger teens (sizes 10–14A), especially those girls with undeveloped busts; juniors (9–15 or 17) for the proportionately short-waisted figure; and misses (10–18) for the normally long-waisted, above five-feet-five figure.

When you are shopping, look out for fit. Make sure that the shoulders fit smoothly, that the waistline of the dress and your own waistline match each other. Look for details such as gaping collars (too large for the neck) and too snug hips. Check the back view; see that the fabric is not all bunched under the arms and above the waistline in back. These all take major alterations, necessitating reshaping the dress. Alterations like sleeve length and hemlines, as well as waistline adjustments, can easily be taken care of, and every teen should learn to do these things herself.

Perhaps you have heard your mother say (and groaned to hear it) that it is better to buy a larger size than a smaller one. You remember too well the awful

days when you were very young and your clothes were bought outsized in the hope that you could grow into them. I'm not advocating a return to such trials, but I do agree with your mother that a too-small dress or suit or coat can never be altered successfully, whereas a large size has a better chance. Clothes can be taken in more easily than they can be let out. You are wiser to buy clothes to fit the biggest part of you (probably your hips) than to fit your smallest part (your waist). Never buy clothes that fit like sausage skins with the intention of losing weight to fit them, or in the hope that you will seem smaller if you wear a smaller size. Instead buy the size that most nearly fits your figure, and then, if there are any adjustments, make them.

If you have really serious difficulty in getting clothes to fit properly (and even if you don't), I think one of the smartest things any teen can do is to learn to make her own clothes. Not only is sewing saving, but your clothes will fit you in every dimension because they are cut to your own individual measurements.

Sewing is not difficult. Most schools offer it in their programs, and it is a wise teen who elects it. You need not, of course, study sewing at school. You can have your mother teach you or, failing that, get instruction from a qualified sewing center. The time you take in learning how to thread a needle and how to master a sewing machine will be repaid many times over in good-looking clothes, well-fitting clothes, and more clothes, because you can usually afford more if you sew at home than if you buy them ready-made.

When you're on the prowl for a new skirt or a new dress, or anything new for that matter, keep your eye peeled on fashion. Follow the trends so that you can know what is on the way in and what is on the way out. If you are clever, you can in this way avoid buying a new outfit and finding out to your horror that it is outdated in a few months. You will do well to watch what goes on in the high-priced fashion field, for those developments are soon copied in the lower-priced clothes, and then you will know what to look for.

But don't go jumping on the fashion bandwagon without a good idea of what you're jumping for. To buy a new outfit just to buy something new because it is new is a poor way to budget. The sooner you learn how to buy what you want when you need it, the faster you'll find that you have fewer difficulties in your wardrobe.

I don't think there's a person alive who hasn't made a mistake at one time or another, who was carried away by something that was just too beautiful to resist, and who subsequently discovered that the dress (or coat or suit) did absolutely nothing for her. Such calamities lie fallow in every closet. But there are ways you can keep your mistakes to a minimum.

Don't buy anything unless it fits your figure, your personality, and your present wardrobe. Consider what you have before you get something new. Try to have the new purchase dovetail into your scheme. Don't switch colors all of a sudden. Switch slowly via accessories and blouses and sweaters so that you can evolve a new color scheme over a period of time without wrecking the one you've already got.

There are times when a bargain turns out to be more than you bargained for, and there are times when it turns out to be a good deal less. A bargain is of no use to you unless it serves a purpose. If you never wear purple, buying a purple dress just because it is cheap is a total waste of money. If you look ghastly in peplums, don't buy a peplum suit just because it's marked down.

Do look before you leap. It is wiser in the long run to buy clothes that make sense than it is to save cents. Good basic costumes in neutral colors should be the backbone of every wardrobe—a wardrobe such as is outlined on P. 57. Allow yourself, at holiday time, at birthday time, when you have a chance to spend your checks or to hint at things you'd like to get, a bit of splurging. But confine your splurging to small items: scarves, blouses, sweaters, jewelry.

These small items put flesh on the basic skeleton of your wardrobe. They add color, they add dash, and they give you a chance to express yourself. Because they are inexpensive, they can be discarded when you are tired of them. Because they are adaptable, they can be changed to suit your fancy. A collection of colorful scarves can pep up a whole closet.

More substantial than accessories, but every bit as switchable, are clothes that mix and match. Sweaters that team up with skirts, jackets that make suits with matching skirts, that look very unsuit-like with contrasting skirts. Blouses that look tailored with school skirts, devastatingly datelike with taffeta skirts. There can be no end to the possibilities of a small collection of separates, provided you have chosen each and every piece with the idea of wearing it with more than one thing you already possess.

The plain fact of the matter is that you are the common denominator of your wardrobe. If you are not divisible into everything you own, then you had better subtract the misfits. A wise girl has few clothes, but clothes that she knows are right and becoming. A foolish girl has lots of clothes, none of which is quite right, and she is always moaning, "But I haven't a thing to wear."

You'll always have something to wear if you plan ahead, if you buy with an eye to the future, a glance at the past, and a firm foothold in the present. It takes practice to straddle three tenses, but it can be done, and the girl who can do it knows that every bit of planning pays off—not only in dollars saved, but in compliments earned.

MARYS' CLOSET

9

What to

Wear Where

It takes a lot of time and a lot of talk to be well dressed—hours are spent on the telephone, in school corridors, around drug store tables, deciding what to wear next Saturday night. But that's as it should be. For unless you keep abreast of the plans you are apt to be surprised. What was once scheduled to be a simple get-together turns out to be a formal dance. A female bridge party at Mary's gets switched to a bring-your-own-date affair. Plans change all the time. It's a wise girl who looks before she leaps—into her closet.

That's why so many of us tend to find out first what others are going to wear

before we make up our minds. And, too, that's why so many of us look exactly alike. But in spite of all our copy-catting, there are those of us who dress well and those of us who don't. The difference lies in how we combine basic ingredients —what sweater with what skirt, colors, accessories, etc.

However, there do exist certain bedrock principles. By and large we have standards of dress that establish what is appropriate and what is not. To be specific, a sweater and skirt are appropriate for school. A black dress is not. You know as well as I do that spike heels are out as far as daytime dress is concerned. The look should be casual. No one goes in for heavy make-up or exaggerated hair styles.

Should you attend a school that requires a uniform, beware of overdressing once you take your uniform off. Don't take out your fashion frustration in cheap jewelry, sequins and ornate glitter. Fads come and go but a simple string of small pearls (good imitations, that is) is still a young girl's best friend.

No smart girl ever lets herself believe that another word for "casual" is "sloppy." Sloppiness, at home or at school, is not to be tolerated. Run-down heels, dirty socks, spot-stained skirts are as much in bad taste as are mascara and strong perfume. Neatness is niceness.

How you look on the street is a question that seldom troubles many of us, yet it is a mighty important one. City officials have been driven to despair by the sight of young ladies traipsing up and down their town in short shorts and bedraggled dungarees. Whether you realize it or not, some so-called "informal" dress is enough to make adult blood pressure rise to the boiling point. For Heaven's sake, have a little pity on others and a lot of pride in yourself; put on a skirt when you're shopping.

For a day's spree in the big city, with lunch and the theatre squeezed into the scheme, you'll want a suit. Wear comfortable, but not play, shoes. Make certain the leather is polished and gleaming. Be sure to remember gloves, a city must. It's nice to have a hat.

Wear a suit to a luncheon party at a friend's house or a restaurant. Perk it up with a pretty blouse or a flower or pin on the collar. A suit, if tailored and in a neutral color, can even change personality with an accessory trick or two. Simple wool dresses, like suits, can go almost anywhere. It's best to have the neckline

high—bare skin is not for daytime.

In summer you can be lots barer and lots less "dressed" than you ever are in winter. Sleeveless cotton dresses are seen everywhere. You can go without stockings, if you choose, provided your legs are free of fuzz and you turn a pretty tan.

When you are uncertain about what to wear, remember that it is always better to be under-dressed than over-dressed. On dates you aren't sure about, wear a suit or a jumper. Add a string of pearls, a flower. Even if you end up at a party where the bunch is decked out in swoopy taffeta, you'll look and feel well dressed.

For casual movie and drug store dates, wear the clothes you'd wear to school—only select from your closet your best or next-to-best sweater instead of that old beat-up affair from three years back. Take extra pains about grooming and pay extra attention to detail.

Don't forget that there are occasions when you must wear a hat. Church is one place where you cannot go bare-headed. Even at an evening wedding you should have a wisp of veiling to cover your head during the service. It is wise to have at least one becoming hat on hand at all times.

Special occasions call for special clothes. A prom, for instance, means an evening dress, more or less bare shoulders, white gloves, evening slippers, and sheer, sheer stockings. To a prom away from home, be sure to remember to pack everything you'll need, including under-skirts and crinoline, and a low-backed bra.

Now is as good a time as any to bring up the difference between "black tie" and "white tie." Both terms, of course, refer to the color of a man's necktie. Black tie, because that is the color worn with a dinner jacket (tuxedo), has come to mean all occasions to which a tuxedo is worn—dinner parties, dances, evening ceremonies. White tie, because white is the necktie color worn with full evening dress (tails), stands for those occasions to which one wears a suit of tails. In spite of the fact that tails are tending to dis-appear more and more from the social scene, they are still the most correct cos-tume for truly formal evening festivities —the opera, balls, weddings. On white tie occasions you should wear your most formal evening clothes.

When traveling, be sure to take clothes of double purpose and quick changeability. A suit is a marvelous com-panion, for it can do so many things— sight-see, go to sporting events, to tea, to lunch. One dressed-up skirt of taffeta, silk or velveteen, that can be worn with a covered-up or a bare necklined blouse is worth its weight in traveler's checks. You can use it for dinner, for dancing, for the theatre, for almost any occasion after five.

When off to a college weekend, make sure that you know in advance the kind of festivities that are planned. Most surely you will want some sort of dress— for a fraternity dance or a special party. You will also need a suit or coordinated skirts and jackets, pretty sweaters, low heels and high heels. You may very well need an evening gown if there is a big dance planned, and you should certainly check on *that* well ahead of time.

In going anywhere away from home, it is wise to know if you'll need any particu-lar equipment—a bathing suit, for in-stance, is a necessity for any girl visiting at the beach. Warm boots, ski pants or slacks are vital to someone off on a winter weekend in the North Woods. Sneakers and shorts should be taken when you know tennis is on the program. A well but not overly equipped guest is tenderly regarded by the hosts who, too often, have had to lend out everything in the house to negligent visitors who failed to think ahead.

It is important to give some considera-tion to the points I have mentioned above. Many people judge us by our dress. Clothes, being such obvious exter-nals, are readily remarked by anyone, and it is, indeed, often our tendency to think of our friends in relation to their dress. "That coat looks just like Mary" or "What a perfect skirt for Jane, just her type."

But being well dressed does not mean dressing expensively or lavishly. Many girls look well and fashionably dressed on very little money—they know how to pick and choose and they have a sure sense of what is appropriate. This "sixth sense" is referred to as "good taste."

Good taste is a difficult expression to define. It is most easily explained as the absence of bad taste, the elimination of the tawdry, the tinselly, the tacky. On the positive side, good taste implies knowing what is suitable for what occasion at whatever time of day. In addition, too, good taste suggests a non-sheep-like attitude, a fillip of daring, an ability to make the individual and personal touch an accepted fashion.

There's an old expression, "Her taste is all in her mouth," which means that the gal in question is lacking in discernment. She's apt to be the kind who wears stage make-up and gobs of jewelry to a casual Saturday night bowling date. She is sure to be fond of extremes—when skirts are long, hers drags the ground; when skirts are short, her knees freeze in the breeze.

Extremes are never in good taste. Avoid, if you can, the flashy and the mousy. Keep a good balance, an equilibrium in all you do.

Below are listed some suggestions for a well-rounded wardrobe:

Lingerie

4 bras—1 black.

2 or 3 panty girdles—that fit.

4 pairs of panties—nylon is your best bet shirred ones give good curve control.

3 or 4 slips—1 black for dark clothes and 2 half-slips (one nylon; one cotton, to starch for wear under full summer skirts).

School

Several basic skirts in neutral shades, some full, some straight. Wool usually wears the best.

Long and short sleeved sweaters in classic colors: beige, gray, navy, green.

1 or 2 jumpers—a good dress-up-dress-down item.

Dates

2 suits—bear in mind that you'll need a suit you can wear to luncheons, teas, and parties now, but which you can also wear as second-best to school later on.

1 basic dress in navy or black taffeta, velveteen or faille.

Formal

1 good formal dress—don't buy it until you need it as styles change rapidly.

1 long or short evening skirt which you can wear with a variety of tops.

Coats

1 camel's hair coat—the perfect cover-all from first class in the morning to late at night. Look for a box cut or flare cut to slip on easily over jackets or sweaters without bunching.

1 light weight topper—to use in warm weather and over evening clothes in winter. Keep to a basic color or you'll tire of it before it's ready for the discard.

1 raincoat—for really sloshy days and to use for hiking and biking trips when you need a covering that can take it.

Note that red, although bright, is an excellent basic color for a coat to be worn anywhere.

Accessories

1 simple string of small pearls (good imitations, unless you're very lucky and have the real thing).

1 pair of pearl button earrings.

1 pair of gold earrings.

1 pair of warm gloves or mittens for school.

2 pairs of white cotton gloves—for dress-up.

1 pair of navy or black gloves.

2 or 3 pairs of nylon stockings—one pair of mesh for school.

Socks to match your sweaters and skirts.

White wool socks for school and sports.

Assorted scarves.

Shoes

Moccasins or saddle shoes for school.
1 pair of pumps in navy or black.
1 pair of evening sandals—either heels or
    flats.

Hats

1 hat each for fall and winter, spring,
    summer—for church, and formal after-
    noon parties.

To Remember

1. Dress down rather than up.
2. Wear clothes appropriate to the occasion—not slacks to Buckingham Pal-
   ace.
3. Never look sloppy outside your own
   room. Be neat.
4. Keep apace with fashion, but don't
   out-distance it. Beware of fads.
5. Pack everything you'll need for visits
   away from home. Make a checklist of
   essential items.

10

Money

(How to
Earn Extra)

"If only I had the money . . ."

The plaintive lament about money or rather the lack of it cannot fairly be said to apply strictly to teen-agers. Many adults and lots of children are afflicted by the same desire. However, teen-agers are in rather a special position in regard to money—they need more of it than children do and yet they are not free to earn it as an adult would.

Some teens, of course, have their own allowances, but sometimes these do not suffice for all the things that need be bought. Mothers and fathers do the best they can to provide for their off-spring's needs, but when it comes to an extra formal or money for a frou-frou blouse, things that aren't desparately needed but desperately desired, then the best answer is to try and earn your own.

Earn your own, you say. All very well, but how? How? In many ways, so many in fact that you can almost take your choice. First you must decide if you want to make money consistently or just in periodic spurts for special expenditures. If you decide that you want a constant supply trickling in every week, then you must find a way that will guarantee a steady income. That is the program I will discuss first.

Jobs that bring in money steadily are jobs at which you must work steadily. Naturally, with school and dates in the picture, these jobs will have to be part-time ones, which can be done of an afternoon or a Saturday. These jobs are not always easy to find, but they do exist. Check into selling jobs in the department store, the drugstore, the stationery shop. Look into waitress jobs, again at the drugstore, the hotel restaurant, and such.

Aside from such steady jobs as these, there are jobs like taking on the sales of magazine subscriptions or greeting cards, which can be steady provided you are willing to devote the time to them.

Baby-sitting can be a steady job or a hit-or-miss affair, depending on the way you want to go about it. If you want to work at it regularly there is nothing to prevent you from making up a list of clients and keeping in constant touch with them. Often young married couples would like to know that they can depend on you to be free to come to their house one definite night a week. You could schedule yourself in such a way, that you could count your chickens in advance.

Such a schedule might look something like this:

> Monday night—The Browns
> Tuesday night—The Smiths
> Wednesday night—The Joneses
> Thursday night—(no regular job)
> Friday night—(no regular job)
> Saturday night—(free for dates)

Don't forget on your schedule to leave room for free time—to do homework, to wash your hair, and for all the million and one things that have to be accomplished. Also, those free nights from time to time can be used to take on emergency jobs when you would like a little extra cash.

Suppose, however, that you don't want to baby-sit on a steady schedule. You only want to do it when you are in a dire financial slump. Then get in touch with a friend of yours who does baby-sit regularly and ask her if she would like to suggest you to her clients as a filler-in. Also, you could baby-sit for friends of your family, on the understanding that you are only free to do it from time to time. However, once you have taken on a job, do not cancel it. Even if you only expect to work spasmodically, you will get yourself a bad name if you back down from an engagement.

In summer baby-sitting can truly evolve into a profitable occupation if during the school months you have established a reputation of being safe and sound. One idea is for two girls to band together to form a sort of unofficial kindergarten. The system would work like this: contact the mothers of five children or so and tell them that you and your friend will agree to take the child in every morning (or every afternoon) five days a week. Think of the boon to busy mothers who would know in advance that all through the summer they could count on three hours or so that would be uncluttered with small children.

In order to amuse the children during the time that you are responsible for them, you could take them to the park, to the playground, or to the beach (if one is nearby). On rainy days you could use your own home (here you would have to talk over the plan with your mother) and read them books and supply them with crayons and paints. With a little organization, you could get the thing going in no time, and incidentally gain some valuable knowledge on the care and feeding of children.

Another kind of activity that can be turned to profit is cooking. If you know your way around a kitchen, you could try and set up a junior catering service. Offer your wares to friends in the neighborhood who you know are planning parties. This is a good summer job, because you have time to do a thorough piece of work and are also free to take on an emergency call. Canvass your block and notify everyone that you will make cakes, cookies, hot rolls, etc., for any parties they are planning. You might also agree to undertake children's parties, doing everything from preparing the cookies and ice cream to making up the games and favors.

Even if you don't cook, other people's parties can be turned to your profit if you offer your services as a helper. You could serve the refreshments, tidy up the house in advance, and clean up afterwards. A few such sessions with mop and dishcloth will enable you to buy that dreamy dress you've long been coveting.

Come summer, you have the time to try out all these schemes. Don't be bashful about starting out. Advertise yourself, ring doorbells, and get going full steam ahead. The idea is to undertake as much as you can, but still have free time to play.

Summer is perhaps the most valuable job time available. It is the time when you can experiment, feel your oats in the business world. Any teen who has a glimmer of what she wants to do when she gets out of school should certainly

try to gain experience in that field some summer before the day of cap and gown. If you yearn to write, go down to the local newspaper and see if they need a copy girl. If you yearn to be a fashion girl, try to get a selling job at the local store (selling experience is one of the surest ways to get ahead in fashion). If you yearn to decorate, see what odd jobs the interior decorator has—remember nothing is too lowly. The way to gain experience is to go out and get it.

Sometimes it is not just an individual who is out of funds; sometimes a whole group, a club or an organization, is down to its collective last dollar. When the exchequer hits bottom with a thud, don't throw up your hands in despair. Instead start figuring out how you can revive the treasury.

Groups can do much to raise money because they have more than one pair of hands to help. What about a raffle, and

why not raffle off Argyle socks made by your own loving hands? Why not raffle off an afghan, with each girl making one square? Why not give a white elephant sale with each member donating some one of her treasures—stuffed animals, old but still useful clothes, etc.?

One of the most enjoyable ways to raise money is to give a party (and charge admission)—but it is also one of the most difficult. In the first place, a party needs money to start off with— money for refreshments, decorations and music (if only records). Perhaps the way to surmount this problem is to have each member of the group contribute— crepe paper from one, one dozen lemons from another, cookies from another, and so on until the list is complete.

One sure way to make a party a success is to invite everyone you know. The more the merrier is a true saying—and furthermore, the more that come, the more admission fees you have to tuck away in the till. Another success tip is ·give yourself time to do the job properly and also time in which to give out advance publicity on your plans. Get oth-

ers excited about what you are proposing to do and they all will come flocking from curiosity.

An unpleasant subject that I am forced to introduce at this point is that often the lack of cold cash is due to mismanagement of funds at hand, otherwise known as poor budgeting. One of the facts of life that must be faced is that money must be handled with sense.

Whether you are on an allowance, whether you earn your own, or whether you come to Mother each time you need cash, you should all know how to budget your money. Budgeting is not mysterious; it is a simple matter of balancing what comes in against what goes out.

One way to set the balance is to estimate your weekly expenses and then try and stay within your estimate. In other words, if your estimate says one movie a week (and that's all you can afford), don't go to a second or you will be certain to run short. Another trick is to save up toward splurges. Put aside a certain amount each week, which later you can spend in one glorious plunge for something you could ordinarily not afford.

One of the most mortal wounds to any budget is to borrow against it with the firm intention of paying it back. You never do. If you can't afford to buy something, don't. If you feel that you really must have whatever it is, then earn extra money, do not borrow, either from your family or from yourself. As I pointed out before, there are easy ways to get quick cash, so you need never complain that you didn't have any other way out.

Sometimes teens want money in sums far larger than those for weekly movies, formal gowns and the like. Some teens need money to pay their way to school or college. It is possible to earn that money if you really keep your nose to the grindstone. Summer jobs become essential—and such jobs as camp counseling are excellent because while you earn you are living free. Your salary is almost net profit.

In fact, any summer job which pays you a salary at the same time that it provides room and board is a sure-fire scheme. In addition to counseling, jobs at summer resorts and hotels, like waiting on table, are highly desirable. If you are interested in this kind of thing make your plans well in advance. You cannot expect to find these positions at the last minute.

There is yet another approach to the art of having enough money, and that is cutting down on expenses—or in the plain parlance of platitudes, "A penny saved is a penny earned." Girls who sew their own clothes will know that for every dress they make instead of buy they have saved and thereby earned a sizable hunk of cash.

Other ways of saving are to ride a bike instead of the bus, write letters instead of making long distance telephone calls, and stay at home and play records instead of feeling obliged to see every movie that comes to town.

A way of saving that will repay you in other ways than cash in the bank is the curtailment of eating snacks between meals. With this method, five cents saved on a candy bar will also be 100 calories saved from settling on your hipline. If you get in the habit of putting in a piggy bank the money that you might have spent on snacks, bus fares, telephone calls, etc., you will be pleasantly surprised to see that at the end of a month you will have earned yourself quite a merry jingle, the sum total of which may surprise you.

It is always easier to save when you are saving with something specific in mind—like saving for a new bike, for a

birthday gift for Mother, for Christmas gifts for the family, for a new anything. It is harder to save just for the sake of saving, but that latter method is a good habit to try and adopt. Try and train yourself to put away mechanically so much each week, to forget in fact that you ever had the money in the first place. Don't even think about it, let it remain in a savings account and grow fat, fatter, fattest, until the day when you really need it for something stupendous.

All in all there is really no reason ever to despair, in this land of ours, for lack of money. If you want a thing strongly enough, you can nearly always find a way to get it. Envy won't produce it, of course, but hard work will—and hard work that can be fun at the same time. No job need seem laborious if you go at it with the intention of having fun. Even mowing lawns can be fun, if you sing at your work—and remember, if you are on a lawn-mowing tour of duty, that you are giving yourself a healthy work-

out that will put zing in your step and slim down your figure.

As a matter of fact, any work that you do, from clerking in a store to washing dishes for Mother, will not only earn you extra cents but will also teach you new facets of life. It will enlarge your horizons, force you to learn patience and perseverance, and better prepare you for the day when you doff the cap and gown and set foot in your own world.

If the lack of a few pennies sets you off to earn your own money, then instead of feeling sorry for yourself you can count yourself lucky, for you are getting your licks in early. There is not one friend of my acquaintance who regrets the time she spent in her school days earning extra money. In fact many of them look to that period as the time when they first learned what stuff life —not dreams—is made of.

Remember that if you have to take a job when you are still in your teens, you may be establishing your career. I never forget that the reason I became a model

was that I needed to earn money for my college tuition.

It is not often that a girl can step right into modeling as a money-making sideline when she is still in school. I was fortunate in that I lived near New York, which is a center of fashion and consequently a place where models are much in demand. It is not often, either, that a girl, having graduated from school, can come to New York, or any other city, and become a success as a model. For every thousand girls who try, I am told, only one succeeds.

It is a strange combination of talents that makes a girl a successful model—a good figure, a photogenic face (one that has interesting planes and angles more than rounded sweetness), an alert air, a great deal of intelligence, and a keen understanding of fashion. Even with all these qualifications, sometimes a girl just doesn't click. The fashion world is fickle.

Because so many teens have asked me how to be a model and what modeling involves, I'll try to sum up the requirements here. For the most part what I have to say will be discouraging. I don't mean to sound hardhearted, but the facts are very bleak.

First, you've got to be ready to work hard. You've got to be prepared to take a lot of hard knocks. I know one young model who has been trying to get established for a year. She is still trying. Recently she told me that she had advised her younger sister, who was thinking of trying her hand also, that the game wasn't worth the candle.

Second, you will need enough money to see you through six months—for in the beginning, jobs, if any, will be few and far between. If at the end of six months you are still ringing magazine's and photographers' doorbells without success, if you have not been taken on by a store or showroom as a regular, then salvage what is left of your nest egg and turn your thoughts to other things. You just weren't cut out to be a model.

As to modeling itself, it is not all made up of posing glamorously for magazines. Many models never even see a camera. These are the girls who work in stores and showrooms (where wholesale dresses are made). They model dresses for prospective buyers. Their life is a round of getting into and out of dresses. They have the advantage, however, of steady work and steady pay. Furthermore, they have the excitement of being in at the beginning of new fashions, for it is in the wholesale showroom (in New York, in Chicago, in St. Louis, in California) where the fashion ideas are born. There the department store people come to buy the clothes you see on the racks. There also come the fashion editors of magazines and newspapers to choose the things they want to photograph and which ultimately you see pictured on their pages.

In addition to showroom models, there are girls who model for department stores—in the expensive salons. These girls are hired on a steady basis, as the wholesale girls are. There are also girls who model for fashion shows, such as stores give from time to time; these girls are not steady employees, but free-lancers. They may do only shows, or they may mix shows with photography.

Then there are models who work only under the lights—the girls who get photographed. Some of them you recognize immediately; their pictures are everywhere. Others, whom you never hear of and hardly ever see, make only enough to scrape along. A photography

is paid only for the number of
he works, and some work only a
rs each month.

Furthermore, a photography model
has a lot of expenses. She has to have
a supply of accessories which may be required by her bookings: such items as
high-heeled pumps, low-heeled shoes,
play shoes, hats, all kinds of gloves. She
also has to be responsible for her cosmetics, lipstick, powder, etc., as well as
always coming to any job with her hair
meticulously groomed. The reason that
the hatbox has become a symbol of modeling is that so many models use it to
carry all this paraphernalia. A model
without her equipment is in just about
the same position as a photographer
without a camera.

There's another kind of equipment
that a model must have, and it's in-
tangible—stamina. It takes stamina to
stand for hours posing under hot lights
in sometimes uncomfortable positions.
It takes stamina to rush from one job
to another without any time between for
a breather. It also takes stamina to keep
to a beauty regimen that will guarantee
success.

How do you get to be a model? I got
to be one by being one. I learned by
watching other models, by studying
poses in pictures, by trying out new
ideas of my own. I learned by listening
to the criticism of photographers and
editors and by profiting by it. Many
models use this system.

Many also have some sort of training
that teaches grace, such as ballet or
dance. Grace is a number-one requirement of a model. A beautiful girl, if she
is awkward, is a failure as a model.
Training is not a requirement, however. I find that many models have never

been near a modeling school. They
model well because they learned by doing.

Also, it must be remembered that a
modeling school cannot guarantee you
success as a model. There are too many
graduates of such schools ever to place
them all in jobs. All that a modeling
school can teach is the fundamental facts
of good grooming, graceful movement
and a bit of the jargon of the business.
From then on you are on your own.

Any girl, model school graduate or no,
starts out the same way. She goes to a
reputable model agency and asks to be
taken on. The agency—if they think that
she has the stuff—will ask to see pictures
(snapshots will do), and will then send
the prospective model off on a tour of
photographers and fashion editors. If
after the tour some of them call the
agency to book her for a job, a career is
under way. If not, there's not much to
be done about it. Signing with an agency
will not get you a job. All the agency can
do is to take your bookings for you, arrange your schedule, send out your bills,
and finally take a cut of your earnings to
pay for its services.

Some models do their own booking,
but that is difficult to manage. It means
that they must have someone to answer
their telephone at all hours, an expensive luxury. They must also make out
their own bills and see to it that they
are paid.

Most models prefer to have an agency
handle the details for them. But they
must always remember that the agency's
function is to take care of their book-
keeping, not to provide them with jobs.

You see, there are a lot of obstacles
in the way of becoming a successful
model—unsteady pay, fickle fashion

(one's face or figure may go out of style overnight), and stiff competition. If you have the makings of a model—thin figure, good bone structure, and grit—then you may get to the top. There are many who would rather not try, and I, for one, don't blame them.

In spite of all the discouraging things I have told you, if your heart is set on trying, then go ahead and try. Just make sure your heart is not overruling your head. Make sure you know what you're doing—and good luck.

11

On the Job

Maybe I'm prejudiced, but I think the working girl who is still a teen-ager and in school often gets overlooked. If it hadn't been for my family and my agency, I doubt that I would ever have learned fast enough how important it is to be as polite and well mannered in business as it is at home. I know from personal experience just what difference those little "Thank you's" and "Please's" can make.

I also learned very early in my working life that no one is indispensable in business. You have to toe the mark to hold a job. This idea of working hard one day and loafing the next doesn't get you very far, believe me. I'm glad I learned all I did so young. It's made my job a whole lot easier. That's one of the reasons I'm devoting a chapter to the subject here.

Many of you who hold part-time jobs probably don't realize just how important those jobs can be. You think of them only as a way to earn extra money—more movies, more vacations, or better educa-

tional opportunities. There's more to it than that. A part-time job can be the beginning of a career. That's why I feel the impression you give makes a big difference.

Good manners are one of the things employers notice right from the very start. By the end of the first working week you will have discovered that manners count every bit as much in the world of the social security card as they do in the world that is just plain social.

A girl who goes to an interview neatly dressed, in a conservative suit or dress, with straight stocking seams, polished shoes, clean gloves and a becoming hat (but not an Easter basket) at once makes a good impression.

Incidentally, I'd like to put in a word here about getting jobs. If you hear of an opening that appeals to you, try to get the name of the executive responsible for filling it. Then write him a brief letter, something like this:

February 12, 19—

Mr. David P. Strong
High Fidelity Insurance Co.
592 Main Street
Houston, Illinois

Dear Mr. Strong:

Mr. Henry Wilkins tells me that you are in need of a new secretary. I am writing to ask you to consider me for this position.

Enclosed is a resumé of my experience and qualifications.

I shall call your office in a few days and ask whether it will be convenient for you to see me.

Respectfully yours,

More about resumés in a minute.

If you don't know the executive, or are writing "blind" to a company you want to work for, address the president. He'll forward your letter to the proper person.

You'll always get an answer to a letter like this. If by some chance you shouldn't, then you should know that the company, or the executive, is too inefficient and impolite for you to waste your time working for.

When you do telephone, the executive or his secretary will have had a chance to know something about you from your resumé and will have an answer ready, either yes or no. You save everyone's time this way. Remember that successful business people are always busy, and few things make them angrier than to be interrupted in the middle of a big deal by a youngster who's just wandered in off the street. Everyone, though, respects an appointment; see that you do too.

A good resumé states your name, address, telephone number and date of birth. It gives your school record, any extra-curricular activities in which you may have participated and any honors you may have received. Any special business skills are listed in full: typing, shorthand, languages, etc. It is imperative that this resumé be neatly typed and well organized. It should be no more than one page.

When you have an interview, whether with the personnel director of the company or with the president himself, be modest but not bashful. Let him know fully and explicitly what you can do, but don't brag. If you've had a job before, suggest that your previous employer was pleased with you and tell any nice things he may have said about you. Also, answer any questions put to you willingly and truthfully. Keep your voice well modulated and distinct. Do not use slang and never be off-hand in your replies.

Unless you're so good and so self-confident that you feel you can pick and choose amongst jobs, never refuse to do anything extra that may be proposed to you. For instance, if you're after a secretarial job and your prospective employer asks if you'd mind helping out with the filing, say you'd be glad to help out. You'll win his heart and you'll get added experience to boot.

Many companies have personnel offices where applicants for positions fill out forms, are interviewed perfunctorily, and then are sent on up to an executive of the company, or are politely told: "We'll let you hear from us." Usually the latter means no soap and you can forget about the place. But be nice to the personnel interviewer, and fill out the form graciously, even if it completely duplicates your resumé. Such people are very skilled observers of human behavior and know far more about you from the way you answer their questions than you could prove with a mountain of papers and recommendations. Don't hedge with them. Remember that even in times of great prosperity there are always at least half a dozen other people waiting for the same job, and if the company is a good one it has thousands more applications than it can possibly fill for a long long time.

After an interview, be sure to write a brief "Thank you" note to your prospective employer, thanking him for the time and trouble he has taken. Follow business form in writing the letter, with the employer's name and firm address in the upper left hand corner, and your name and address in the lower right. Do this regardless of whether you get the job or not; it might tip the scales in your favor.

Once you are hired, don't relax your efforts. Be sure to report to work neatly dressed, with your make-up in low key. Remember that your looks will be judged by those around you. It is especially important to be scrupulously careful of your appearance if you are working at a job where you come in contact with a firm's customers, for your appearance will reflect on the firm. Salesgirls, waitresses, receptionists all know this.

Courtesy on the job is mighty significant. You must be as polite towards fellow employees as to customers. On the telephone, be distinct and cheerful. Have an eager-to-please note in your voice. When answering, be sure to follow the formula approved by your firm. "Hello" is not a usual business technique. Never keep anyone waiting long—if you leave the phone to get information, be certain to ask the person to hold on a few minutes, please. If there is a long delay, ask if you may call back.

In direct face-to-face conversations, have a smile and an interested expression for the customer. Don't look bored or irritated—sure, your feet may hurt, and you may have a headache, but in business you have to keep on smiling. (It's a good practice in private life too. Inflicting your ills on others can become awfully tiresome.)

A willingness to please is one of the biggest assets a young girl can have. Sincerity, genuine interest in people, a natural ease in conversation, honesty, all do much to make a young person a truly delightful individual—on and off the job.

Always remember that the time you spend at work is time for which you are being paid for service rendered. Never fall into the careless habit of thinking that you need do only as little as you can to get by. It is important to be businesslike in your thinking, to take the attitude that all that you learn can and will be of value to you.

If you work hard, you will not have the time to bring personal affairs into business conversation. Don't do it anyway! Stay off the office telephone. Be back on time after your lunch hour. No excuses that you were held up by your steady beau. Keep a clear head and an honest heart and you'll have a fine time.

To Remember

1. Be neatly and conservatively dressed for business.
2. Have a prepared resumé ready before going in to see a prospective employer, or, better, mail it first with a letter asking for an appointment.
3. Thank, in writing, each person who has interviewed you for a job.
4. Be constantly courteous to co-workers, to the public you serve.
5. Never treat a business office as if it were your private boudoir.

12

Look Pretty—Be Pretty

Not so long ago I knew a very pretty girl who had come to New York to be a model. She ought to have been a sure-fire success. But oddly enough she didn't catch on. At first I couldn't figure it out. She was lovely to look at, modeled well in front of the camera and took excellent photographs. Then, one day, when I was working with her at the same booking, I found out what the trouble was. She was unpleasant. She complained about the lights, about the clothes, about the poses. Nothing satisfied her. She had a permanent chip on her shoulder. Small wonder that photographers, editors and everyone else in the fashion business did not want to work with her.

You see, good looks are not enough. In order to be a success in this world, you have to *be* pretty as well as *look* pretty. How do you get to be pretty? By having

a pleasant personality. Sounds simple, but it isn't. For a pleasant personality means that you must be affable, considerate, generous, open hearted and polite, adjectives that add up to good manners.

Good manners are not just an artificial formula. They are actually ways of expressing our good feelings and intentions. Without them, even with the best will in the world, we appear to be rude. Lots of us don't often stop to think about that. We tend instead to lump good manners with formality and consider the whole thing as something deader than seventeenth century court etiquette. That's where we are wrong. For modern manners have nothing in common with Louis XIV.

Modern manners are up to date, as informal as the age we live in. We don't fuss and fret about minor rules and regulations — whether, for instance, a boy escorting two girls should walk in the middle or at the curb side of the street (old fashioned propriety says the curb side, a hang-over from the days when the male was there to protect the female from highway dangers like runaway horses, mud splashes, etc., but moderns prefer the easy amiability of the middle.) We are more concerned about basic fundamentals.

The most basic of all the basic fundamentals is getting along with people. You can't have fun all by yourself. You need to share pleasure in order to really savor the sensation. That means having friends. In order to have friends, you must be the kind of person people like, and to be that kind of person you must have those qualities which are likable.

It's as plain to me as the nose on my face that if we don't behave nicely, how is anyone to know that we are nice? If we don't show love and respect for our family, how are they to guess? Alas, too many of us think that we can do as we please and that people will take us for what we are. Somewhere we have got the mistaken idea that polite phrases are unnecessary sugar coatings, useful only to get us out of jams. We've scrapped "Please" and "Thank You" on the junk heap of human relations.

Sunday best manners aren't enough. Everyday courtesy is what counts. What we say and do at home, at school, at work and at play is what makes us nice to have around or just a nuisance.

Think of the family, for a minute. How tough do we make things for Mom and Dad every once in a while? It's not, of course, that we mean to be nasty, but we just don't stop to look and listen. We jump in with both feet and often

they wind up in our mouths.

Now Mom may sometimes seem sort of old fashioned and a little behind the times, but her advice is meant for the best. She loves you, and because she loves you she tries to help. Sometimes it seems that she's butting in where she doesn't belong, but she certainly doesn't mean it that way. Try to see her point of view. Consider for a second that what she tells you is for your own good.

Same goes for brothers as well. Take my brother Bob, for example. Now, goodness knows, Bob was the kind of brother who delighted in correcting me (still does, for that matter). He took a personal interest in my affairs. One of his favorite tricks was "third degreeing" my new dates with remarks like "You're new around here, aren't you?" I could have sunk right through the floor whenever that happened. I thought that Bob was just trying to be mean. It never occurred to me that he was looking out for my best interests by sizing up my new beaux. Of course, now I know better.

Although you understand the protective feeling that comes over big brothers from time to time, it often doesn't help matters much when your date gets that "What comes off here?" look cast at him. Maybe it would be a good plan to ask Bob to go easy on the guys until they are more at ease in your home. If you ask nicely, he'll see things your way and he'll go about his "duty" more subtly. Remind your older brothers that much as you appreciate their interest in your young men, you don't want to see your dates scared off the reservation. And vice versa. If Bob keeps hands off your men, you keep hands off his girls.

Look behind the things that people say to find out what they are all about. Especially with your own family. We live so closely with our families that we tend to have a poor perspective. Relationships get out of focus. The very proximity of each member of a family to the others occasionally starts the trouble.

No one in this day and age of progressive education and belief in the importance of the "individual" is going to ask you to behave in the manner once prescribed for the "perfect little lady," but people do expect you to be fair and square. Grumblers and complainers make things tough for every member of a household. Sure, it isn't easy to be sweet and obliging when your plans have gone all wrong and you feel that your parents have acted unreasonably, but you can make an effort. Get a good grip on your temper and hold tight. You'll find that you can ride out many a tantrum with a dry eye and calm countenance.

Getting along at home becomes a problem only when you make it one. Try taking the attitude that perhaps some of the friction is your own fault. Did you ever stop to think that maybe you expect too much of your family? With the same nonchalance that you accept a bed, breakfast and clean clothes, you take for granted kindliness, understanding and love. That's going a little far.

Try telling your parents how much you love them. Let them know you appreciate all they do for you. Words are wonderful emotional bridges. Thank Mom and Dad from the bottom of your heart for their support and encouragement. Sure, they know without your saying that you love them for what they do, but your saying so actually helps. Put yourself in their shoes. How would you feel day after day to have no sign that your efforts were appreciated?

Take some time out from your own problems to consider what burdens your parents must carry. Small wonder that now and then Dad is irritable. He has the responsibility for the family on his shoulders. Have you thought about that, or have you dismissed him as an old bear because he tells you that you wear too much lipstick and that you come home too late at night? Have you thanked him recently for his advice (whether you asked for it or not), or did you snappily retort that it wasn't any of his business? Are you giving Dad a break?

Are you playing fair with Mom? Do you draw into a shell when she asks you about a date? Have you considered that she was a girl like you once and knows more than you would ever guess about the torments that go on in your heart? After all, she's a woman the same as you, only older, busier. But like you she likes and needs to get compliments, affection and pretty presents. Do you do your part?

You're not doing your part if you behave as though your parents were put on earth solely for your convenience. Remember that you are only a fraction of the total family circle. Stick to your fair share of the circumference.

Some girls just never seem to be able to figure out how much of the circle is theirs. They are bright enough in geometry class, but pretty dumb in manners. Take, for example, one girl I used to know — I'll call her Sally.

When Sally wanted to use the telephone, nobody else could get near it. In Sally's eyes Alexander Graham Bell had invented that instrument just for her special convenience. Too bad for Mom! Too bad for Dad! In desperation they were driven to the phone booth in the corner drugstore. The radio and the TV set also were tuned to what Sally wanted

to hear and see. Sunday funnies found their way pronto to Sally's room, and so did the last piece of cake, and the new lending library book.

Really, when you think about it, you can't blame parents for getting fed up once in a while. It's easy to see that there are times when family friction owes its first fiery sparks to you. More care and consideration on your part would do much to smooth over little difficulties.

On the other hand, it is true, you have a point when you say: "Being sweet doesn't solve everything. I can't make my parents understand me. They don't see that some things are private. They snoop."

Where privacy is concerned I'm on the side of every girl who has ever kept a diary. There certainly are some things that belong to you alone, experiences that the very thought of sharing makes you turn inside out.

Among the things that I believe you have a right to keep from prying eyes are mail, secrets and personal papers. They belong to you and you alone. However,

you will find that if you are honest with your parents, they will respect your right of privacy and will not violate it. What drives many families to pry is the feeling that they know nothing about your life. They are afraid of things you may have done and their fears force them to find out — and so they pry.

The way to work out a solution is to tell your family something about yourself, what you think, how you feel. Bring your friends home for them to meet and you will discover that in those areas that are strictly private, they will leave you alone. That works both ways too. If you open up your heart to your family, they will open up to you. You will both benefit by sharing ideas and opinions.

Nothing pleases a parent more than to be asked for advice. Nothing gives an older brother or sister a bigger boost than to be thanked for a suggestion. Nothing sets you up better with a younger brother or sister than taking an interest in what he or she is doing. It's all so simple. Everyone likes to feel important, and you imply how important they are to you by showing that you care about things they do and say.

Beware of letting a love of privacy spill over into selfishness. It's not asking much to think first before we gripe, to consider the other fellow. Putting "Please" and "Thank you" at the front or at the end of our sentences may seem like a little thing but it adds up to a lot. Sometimes it makes all the difference.

What works at home, works at school. And in both instances there is nothing that a little courtesy won't cure. Of course it's easier to say something about this than to do something about it. Especially at school. At school we are involved in a situation that is bigger than just the individual. Our actions are in-

fluenced by what the crowd does. It takes a lot of fortitude to act on a personal basis.

Most teens I know are afraid of being "greasy grinds." They are even afraid of being associated with greasy grinds. Believe me, I was one who disliked immensely that fellow with brains, the guy who always carried a brief-case and who hit the books every night. I remember chemistry class. I sat opposite Frank and did all the lab experiments with him. He knew all the answers, but he had few friends. He didn't have time to date much and never got in with a crowd. Most of the kids were jealous of his grades.

One day Frank asked me for a date. I said I was sorry but I was booked up. He asked me again and again. Finally I had to say yes. I wasn't very pleased about it and I guess I showed it. Well, anyway, Frank arrived at the house, and without his brief-case and glasses he was a terrific fellow. I kicked myself all over the block for having been such a dope and taken so long to find out that outward appearances can be awfully deceiving.

It isn't easy when you're in school to make a decision for yourself. Sometimes, as it happened to me, you do all you can to avoid having to make one, but sooner or later the time comes. I think you owe it to yourself to establish your own code of decent behavior so that when you are face to face with a problem you can solve it with honesty and good taste.

How should you go about making up a personal code? As I see it, respect for the individual should be at the top of the list. Respect is a word that more and more seems to be disappearing from our lives. We've just about given it up in our relationships with our parents, and it is pretty nearly nil in our attitudes to teachers and administrators. It's time, I think, we gave the matter some serious thought.

In the first place, parents and teachers are worthy of respect. The very fact that they are adults and hold down responsible jobs qualifies them for some attention. To parents, of course, we owe much more than respect; we owe them love and understanding. But teachers have little else to go on. It is up to us to see to it that the job they do is made as easy as possible for them. How would you like to teach a class that is looking out the window, combing hair, chewing gum and passing notes? I'll bet you wouldn't get much of a kick out of it.

A good teacher would be the last person in the world to ask you to pretend to do something you don't believe in. You don't have to fake friendliness for a person you don't admire, but you should behave kindly and politely toward that person. Keep your feelings to yourself. Cutting remarks can have a double edge. There's no guarantee that you won't find yourself bleeding along with your victim.

Above all be fair and honest. Cheating weakens your character. There is no such thing as a little of it. Whether you cheat in exams or cheat in sports, it all boils down to the same thing. That's what so few of us understand. Those of us who never under any circumstances think of being underhanded in athletic activities, will copy somebody else's homework without a twinge of conscience. I have no illusions that this little book will be able to tell you what to do when you are confronted with cheating — either as to the person who wants information, or as the person who gives it; but I do hope that my pointing out the problem will remind you that it is a subject that cannot be airily dismissed. You've got to think about it.

Do let me say, though, that having a reputation for being a good sport — and by that I mean a person who is completely above board, a person who wins well and who loses well — is worth trying for. It is a great quality and one that will stand you in good stead everywhere. Good sportsmanship is one of the meas-

ures of good conduct the world over.

As a good sport you know what is expected of you. You take victory with generosity, and defeat with good will. You never hint that the other team did anything but their best and you accept any decision of the referee. Booing is beneath you. Nobody cheers harder than you do for your home team, but when the game's over, there should be no hard feelings.

When you can look at life without rancor, you have gone a long way toward being a mature person. Don't think that yon need to turn into a teacher's pet. Nothing is farther from the truth. Polishing the apple never made anybody into a better person. It's polishing yourself that does the trick. Some of the process may seem rough to you — like smiling when you feel like crying, and being nice when you'd rather knife — but the rewards are so terrific that it's worth all the effort you can spend.

13

Are You Shy?

Shyness is an experience that most of us have had at one time or another. Some of us get over it quickly, like the measles, but others find that it drags on and on like a bad cold. Whichever way it hits you, it's a tough thing. You feel constantly ill at ease and cut off from the world. You'd like to come out of your corner, but you're frightened. There's a big lump in your throat, and you know that if you try to express the thoughts inside, you'll break down and cry.

Oh, I know what people say — that you should make yourself talk, go to parties, join in conversations and get out and go, but it isn't as easy as all that. Advice and action are two different things altogether. Nonetheless something's got to be done, because you're missing all the fun. Well, I have found a few remedies that seem to work.

First off, I think the most important thing about getting over shyness is to do it by degrees. Start small and work up. Set yourself a daily task such as answering the telephone or the door-bell, two situations that put you in touch with people. Keep at that until you feel comfortable and un-selfconscious. Then branch out to bigger things, like joining a club where you will be thrown in with a group of people your own age who share your interests.

Most helpful in combating shyness are good manners. When you say and do the right things you feel at ease. I have found that even if you perform certain courtesies by rote, they help to get you over the rough spots. Take the simple matter of "Hello" and "Good morning." If you get yourself to greet your friends and acquaintances with these ordinary formulas, you'll discover that lots of ice is broken. "Please" and "Thank you" do much the same.

Shyness has an advantage that in our misery we tend to overlook. When we're shy, we become sensitive to other people. We are aware of personal problems and heartbreaks that others never sense or see. Because of that sensitivity, we can be more sympathetic and open hearted — but only if we force ourselves to communicate that understanding. Very helpful in communication are formulas of politeness: the thank-you note, the congratulatory note, the note of condolence. By following a cut and dried pattern dictated by form, we can lose our self-consciousness, yet at the same time express our sincere feelings. Never be hoodwinked into thinking that because a formula is a formula it need be without meaning. One genuine "Thank you" means more than a carload of superficial compliments.

It is important to remember that when you are shy it is possible for you to give people the impression that you are rude. Because you find it difficult to express yourself, you often don't try. Your failure to give of yourself can be, and sometimes is, interpreted by others as selfishness and lack of interest. That's why I feel you will save yourself lots of misunderstandings if you rely on form. Let your more articulate friends think up fancy ways of saying things; you stick to basic principles until you have gained social confidence.

So many teens think that shyness is something to be ashamed of. Heaven forbid! What would the world be like if everyone were a Goodtime Charlie? Visualize a party where everybody wanted the spotlight — chaos! Thank your lucky stars that there are a few people who would rather listen than lecture. Of course I admit that all of us sooner or later have the feeling that it must be fun to be the center of attention, but just remember that more often than not it's the girl who can sit quietly and admire the antics of the big shot who ends up with her man. The normal male likes nothing better than someone to tell him he's wonderful, someone who isn't vying with him for attention. The Southern belles didn't get their fame by virtue of an eighteen-inch waist alone. They knew the secret of tranquility.

Still, knowing what the compensations are does not actively help when you are confronted with an agonizing situation. What, for instance, does one do when plopped down beside an absolute stranger. Talk — yes — but what about? Well, my answer is anything under the sun: the weather, the latest movie, last night's TV program, a football game. By and large, it is a good thing to keep the subject vague and general. You are not likely to strike a person who wants to hear about fish breeding or advanced algebra.

If you're lucky, a little digging will produce results and your partner, unless he too is shy, will pick up the conversational ball and dribble on down field. All you have to do then is see to it that you nod yes and no in the right places, keep an interested look on your face, and ask a few questions.

Next to wanting to know how to begin a conversation, a lot of my friends want to know how to get out of one. They've been stuck in a corner for an hour and they can't get away. Is there a graceful

way to make a get-away? Yes, there is. Wait for a break in the monologue, then murmur something about having to speak to someone in another part of the room. Say you're so sorry to have to go, how much you've enjoyed hearing about his sailboat, but you promised to help with the dishes. Or, you can retire to the little girls' room (with excuses) and wait until he has found another victim.

It's not wise to break up a conversation — even with the deadliest bore — unless you are certain you can do it gracefully. Better sit and suffer than hurt somebody's feelings. You wouldn't want your own hurt, would you? And remember that though in your opinion the guy is duller than a rubber knife, his own friends like him, and they will resent your attitude — rightfully. You might easily find your-

self the subject of some unpleasant remarks on their part.

If you are new to a crowd or a community, it is often difficult to feel part of a group. Everything seems strange and forbidding. The best way to handle the situation is to wait it out. After a while you will begin to catch on to local customs. Slowly the kids at school and the neighbors down the street will take you in. Don't force it, but let it come gradually. It helps to join school clubs and community projects — the Y, the Red Cross, church clubs, etc. Or get a part-time job, or take up a hobby or a sport.

The biggest thing about shyness is not to let it get you down. No matter what comes, don't draw into your shell. If you keep smiling, you'll find that much of what you fancied to be hurts and slurs are really only in your own imagination. Closing in your circle only makes you prey to day-dreaming in which you over-emotionalize your life. Keep busy and you won't have time for self-pity.

I started modeling when I was still in school. The minute classes were over for the day, whoosh — into New York to work. I never had much time to call my own, but believe me, I never regretted it. My days were so full that I had no leisure to fuss and fume. Consequently I found that the problems I thought I had to face simply weren't there — they had disappeared before I ever found an opportunity to mull them over. Furthermore, the more you do to fill your free time the more you'll find yourself coming into contact with people, and the easier it will be to make yourself at ease.

14

It's a Date

You've got a date, you're going out, and you're not fretting your pretty little head over anything except perhaps the problem of what you are going to wear.* Far be it from me to poke holes in your pink cloud, but there are a few points that I'd like to remind you of.

First and foremost, once you have made a date, keep it. The only excuse for breaking a date is the unforeseen occurrence of a crisis in your family, sickness, death or change of plans — Mom and Dad decide to go away for the weekend or to include you in a project which they have at hand — theatre, visit, etc. Obviously, in such instances, your parents' desires come first and you must tell

your date so — giving him the honest reason why you have been forced to cancel out.

But if you have no good reason to break a date, other than your own wish to do so, then you should not. Indeed, good manners demand that you must not. Even if it means turning down a chance to do something else you would much rather do, you have got to stick with your original agreement. You have given your word and should not go back on it. Furthermore, the boy you first accepted and then turned away is going to find out sooner or later that you broke your date with him to go out with another boy. Believe me, he is not going to be one little bit pleased. You've hurt his pride

* For suggestions, see Chapter 6.

(a breach of good manners and under any code a most unfeeling way to behave), and who is to blame him if he tells all his friends that you're a stinker. As for the boy you picked in preference, he may be flattered that you broke a date to accept him, but deep down he will be somewhat suspicious of you, afraid that you'll pull the same trick on him some day. Coming and going, you've gained nothing by your cavalier behavior, save a reputation for not being trustworthy.

Much better is it from the very beginning to refuse a date that you know you may not want to keep. There are ways to accomplish this gracefully, without hurting anyone's feelings. All you need to do is to sound genuinely sorry that you must say no, suggesting that you have already made other plans. If the boy is the kind who does not name a date, but simply

says hopefully, "When are you free?" I admit the problem becomes more thorny. In that case, there's not much you can do but say that for the time being you are fairly heavily booked up and your parents think you ought not to accept any more engagements. If that doesn't work, nothing will — if the poor guy can't take a hint, well, you are stuck with having to give him a firm "no."

When a boy calls you for a date, say yes or no, don't hem and haw. Teasing is not nice. Nobody likes to be kept dangling. For my money, the deadliest female menace of all time is the girl who first must find out all the details — where they will go, whom they will see, etc., — before she will give her answer. You'll be behaving in a much more intelligent and lady-like fashion if you make your decision without first fishing to find out what is involved. You can always ask afterwards what sort of plans he has in mind, so you may know how to dress. Never forget that it is both polite and smart to let a boy think you have accepted a date because of the boy himself, not because of the good things he can offer.

What to do about a blind date? You hesitate to say yes right away for fear of being stuck. You are, I agree, in a ticklish spot. My advice is to say yes when you trust the person who is making the arrangements. In spite of the fact that the unknown boy may turn out to be a flop, you at least know the other couple involved. After all, it is only one night in your life. You can suffer a bit to do a friend a favor. If, on the other hand, you are asked to go by people you know only slightly, you are perfectly free to refuse. Politely, of course. But, a word to the wise, don't be afraid of blind dates. Even if the boy is awful, he may have a friend who is divine.

Speaking of dates, stick to your own, unless you want to lose one of your best girl friends. Even if her beau asks you (and you know she's crazy about him) be diplomatic and tell him "No." Because not only will she be an unfriendly friend, the other girls can and will get mighty catty. If you do like him, and he you, be patient and wait till her romance blows over. If he's sincere he'll ask again in a month or two.

Assuming that you have said "yes" to the boy who has asked you for a date (and that I think is a fair assumption for most of us) don't forget to be ready at the appointed time. No boy — repeat — *no* boy likes to be kept waiting. It is, I assure you, boys' biggest peeve. Be downstairs and ready to go to the door when the bell rings. Do remember to introduce your date to your parents, if they have not already met. That last admonition is important. It is very rude to waltz out of the house with a boy whom your family has never laid eyes on.

Once out the door, a date begins in earnest. What, oh what, some of you ask, do we talk about at this moment? Anything under the sun. Talk about school, sports, television, movies, any subject which you think will spark his interest. You wouldn't start with butterflies, unless you happened to know in advance that your date is devoted to them, but you might choose basketball or bathing suits. The "b's" are full of possibilities, as are the other twenty-five letters in the alphabet. If you are shy and hate to make the first move, plan something ahead to get the ball rolling. A question is good, since you can sit back and listen to the answer. Try something like "Did you see the game yesterday?" or "What do you think of so-and-so on TV?" Your date is bound to have some opinion. Encourage him to express it.

Chances are that you will be out on a double date, so the burden of conversation won't be up to you alone. Do make sure, though, that you don't flunk your responsibility. Keep interested in what is going on. Throw in a comment when there is a pause or lag. Try to keep yourself somewhere between the two unpleasant extremes of the chatter-box who never lets another get a word in edgewise; and the silent mouse who can't even muster up a squeak all evening long.

One important thing to remember on a double date is to keep the conversation general. Don't spend all your time talking to one person, the other girl, your date — or worse, her date. Consider what it means to the others to be left out. Two people on a double date who cross-talk constantly between themselves make others feel uncomfortable and unwanted.

It's so easy to bring everybody into the conversational circle. A "Don't you think so?" or "How do you feel about it?" will do the trick.

For Heaven's sake, in your search for a topic to talk about, don't fall back on gossip. If you only knew how boys squirm when they hear two girls going at it tooth and nail, you'd never utter another "You'll never guess what I heard . . ." again. Cattiness cuts two ways. You may knife your own back in the bargain.

It is absolutely against all decent standards of behavior to discuss one date with another. Positively, it is not done! Never say to Johnny, "Really, Jimmy is an awful bore, a real dope." Never say to Jimmy, "Johnny lets me do what I please when he takes me out." Whether you praise or blame, comparisons, either stated or implied, are not in good taste — anywhere, at any time.

Implicit in all good behavior is the fact that you never embarrass anyone if you can possibly avoid it. On a date, never put a boy in a position where he feels foolish. Don't ask to go somewhere he can't afford. Don't wear loud clothes, or sloppy clothes. Be quiet and controlled in public places. Don't scream and yell in a car, on a bus, in the subway, on the street. Don't be conspicuous in the movies, at a restaurant, anywhere you may be that is not within the confines of your own home.

Too many of us in an effort to take the spotlight go through all kinds of contortions to make people look at us. It's a silly thing to do. We are only making fools of ourselves. No boy wants his date to be laughed at, or to be the cause of annoyance to those around. And that is exactly what happens when you behave badly. You may think it is cute — acting the cut-up on the main street — but it is really only tiresome.

There are some girls who think they are being coy when they taste the food and drink that others have ordered. "Let me try that." "Oh, that looks good, give me some." If they only knew what pests they are to the others around them, they'd stop soon enough. It is an awful bore to have to put up with someone who is being desperately "cute."

Consideration for others is the biggest part of good behavior. But you have to stop and think about it. It may not seem like very much to you, but four teenagers coming down the street abreast, talking at the top of their voices, is enough to send older pedestrians scattering for cover. Two kids in the back seat of a bus who start a friendly rough-and-tumble can put the rest of the passengers on pins and needles for the remainder of the ride. A table of chattering school girls in a drug store can, if they forget where they are and begin to raise their voices, make other shoppers forget what they came in to buy. There are people who no longer go to the movies because they can't stand the yells and jeers, or the rows and rows of high-school students who think that the theatre is theirs to do with as they please.

Part of growing up is a realization that whatever you do has an effect on others around you. When you were a child you were excused for misbehavior. Now you are not. So wise up to yourself and act your age. You could attract the center of attention when you were three by standing on your head in the grocery store, but you're too old now for such acrobatics — and when you think about it, isn't it just as well?

What we are looking for, now that we are older, is to have a good time ourselves and to let others have a good time. That's why we should think first of our date and put his wishes foremost. That's why we don't flirt with other boys when we are out with one boy. We pay strict attention to our own date — not smothering him with sticky sentiment, but making him feel that for this evening it's he that we care about. That's why a girl should always tell her date at the end of the evening how much she has enjoyed it.

Good manners make it easy for a girl to let a boy feel master of any situation. In a restaurant it is the boy who pays, who gives the order for the two of you to the waiter, who makes arrangements for the table. Even if you have agreed to go Dutch, you can give your date your share of the bill later, in private. At the movies, if you want to pay your way, it is easy enough to give the boy your ticket money beforehand, inconspicuously.

Be easy and natural in your relationship to your date and to others around you. Don't criticize or nag. Swearing is not smart. Don't be fooled into thinking that profanity or vulgarity makes you seem like a big time operator.

A girl with good manners never lets her date wait for minutes on end while she chatters away in the powder room with her pals. Or makes him languish while she runs off to talk to a friend. A nice girl never puts a boy on a spot. Never teases or pokes fun at him so that he feels conspicuous and ridiculous.

Scenes in public places, for any reason at all, are beyond the pale. No matter how angry you get, you must control your temper until you get within the privacy of your own room. There you can steam like a tea kettle until you get it all out of your system. Fights, physical or verbal, may never be conducted in full view of the public eye. Even if your date has done you dirt, left you stranded beyond all decency, you must not make others uncomfortable by publicizing your predicament. If you find yourself in such a situation, seek out the boy and tell him you want to go home. If he refuses (a sign that he is boorish anyway) call your parents and ask them to come and fetch you. Leave quietly and keep your peace. Putting the shoe on the other foot — a girl must never desert her date to the point that she abandons him and goes home with another boy.

It is not always easy to be well behaved at all times. So often you get carried away by the fun you are having, you raise your voice, fling yourself around, get giddy with excitement. That's all very well and good provided that down deep you always remember to be considerate toward others. It is not possible to be meek and mild all the time, but it is possible to be kind and thoughtful. If you think that you have got out of hand, you should always make excuses later. You can say later to your date: "Johnny, I hope I wasn't too noisy last night. I didn't realize how loud I was talking." Or you can call your neighbors and say: "Gee, Mrs. Brown, I hope that I didn't bother you last night. I am afraid we were a bit noisy when we drove up. There was an awful crowd in the car," and so on. People will appreciate your thoughtfulness, even if the damage has already been done.

Petting is not properly a subject for a chapter on good manners. There are, however, aspects of petting that do concern us. Whether or not you pet, how far you go is your own private problem. However, once you are in a public place, what you do becomes a matter of public concern. No one wants to go to the movies and observe the antics of a loving couple in the row ahead. No one wants to go to a diner and eat a hamburger seasoned with the simpering goings-on of two moonstruck youths. The minute you go beyond holding hands in public you have gone too far. Embraces and kisses which are carried on for all the world to see are in poor taste.

It is obvious, too, that a girl who is lavish with her affection to any and all comers is hardly a girl who commands much respect. She is a girl for whom boys will not feel the need of exhibiting their own good manners, so that she often asks for the trouble she gets herself into. That's why good manners suggest that a girl keep a "hands off" attitude until she is sure she has found someone she truly cares about. When she thinks herself honestly in love and she's old enough to be a judge of her emotions, then what she decides to do is purely personal. However, she must always remember that public display of affection (even to a fiancé) is never, never done.

To Remember

1. Never break a date, once made, unless a family crisis comes up.
2. Don't make a date feel uncomfortable by any word or action.
   a. You must not cause him to "lose face" in any manner or you will automatically forfeit his respect.
3. Keep conversation general — don't gossip or devote your attention to just one person if there are more than two of you involved.
4. Be quiet and considerate of others.
5. Apologize if you have over-reached yourself.
6. Never pet in public.

15

Going Formal

A pretty dress, all skirt and no shoulders, tiny slippers, a sparkling jewel, tidy white gloves, all these laid out on the bed are a sure sign that there's a big dance in the offing. There's excitement in the air, and the rustle of tissue paper. The bathroom is damp with steam — you've never been cleaner in your life. It's hard to believe that after waiting so long, the evening has come at last. You've been building up to this moment ever since you got that wonderful telephone call from Jimmy: "Will you go to the dance with me on Friday?"

All through dinner you fidgeted, wondering if you should try a new hair-do but, over dessert, finally decided against it. And now suddenly here you are, all dressed and ready. Wise girl! You know that Jimmy should not be kept waiting, that it's a silly conceit to make men stand around in order to foster the illusion that their dates are not over-anxious.

Probably Jimmy has brought you a corsage. If so, you thank him very genuinely for his selection even if it clashes with the color of your dress. Then and there you pin it on to show him how pleased you are, perhaps tucking it in your hair, or at your wrist if you think the colors are too opposed to look well on the dress itself. Otherwise you pin it to your right shoulder so that it won't get crushed while dancing — which is what happens to fragile flowers that are fastened on the left side. If you decide the corsage belongs on your shoulder, pin it on with the stems down — the way flowers grow.

Maybe Jimmy had the foresight when he called to ask you what color dress you were planning to wear, so that he might choose his flowers accordingly. If so, he showed a very high degree of courtesy and you should mention it in your thanks. If he did not ask, you should not tell him openly, for it is not polite to indicate your wishes in the matter, no more than it is right to fish for a compliment. A corsage is, after all, a gesture of courtliness and affection — it should not be thought of as your rightful due. It should be considered a gift. It is rude beyond belief for a girl to criticize a corsage or to suggest in any way that the flowers are not up to expectation.

After taking leave of your parents, you depart for the dance. No doubt you have already been told the hour at which you are expected back. Jimmy, too, has been made aware of his parents' wishes in the matter. Be honest to each other at the beginning about what is expected of each of you and make your plans accordingly.

If the dance is one that has a receiving line, you are expected to go down it together. Jimmy waits for you to take off your wraps in the room set aside for that purpose, and if you must do a last minute make-up job, be quick about it. Don't keep him waiting.

There is nothing forbidding about a receiving line. Besides, Jimmy will be right behind you — you go down the line together. You have only to shake hands with everyone, smile sweetly, say "How do you do," and go on. You are not expected to start up a conversation. (This is true of any receiving line, even that of a wedding, though at such a time you may want to expand your greetings to include some mention of how pretty the bride is.)

To the first person in line, give your name in a simple and natural fashion, saying: "How do you do. I'm Mary Jones." The first person will then turn you over to the next in line, simultaneously repeating your name. This goes on until you have reached the end of the chain. It is quite probable that by the last handshake your name has become Miss Sauerkraut, but that is not important.

Should you know the first person in line, you have only to say: "How do you do." It is not necessary to give your name, since that is already known to the receiver.

Should you recognize the person as a family friend, yet someone who does not know you, it is correct and polite to say: "How do you do. I'm Mary Jones, Walter Jones' daughter."

The receiving line completed, you are free to get on to the dancing. Your first dance is obviously reserved for your date, as is the last. After that, all sorts of systems may prevail. If it is to be a card dance, where the dances are numbered and are given out to those who request them, then you dance with those with whom you have made arrangements. If, as is a general practice nowadays, there are no set arrangements, you are free to dance with all comers.

Cut-ins are a general rule nowadays

and boys should expect to be cut-in on. From time to time, it is evident, the girl should see to it that she is giving her escort some of her attention. If she catches his eye while he is standing about forlornly in the stag line, she should encourage him to come back and cut in. After all, her first responsibility is to him.

A girl at a dance should expect to dance with strangers. It is perfectly correct to have a young man come up and introduce himself and ask for the next dance. The girl, if she is free and likes his looks, accepts and gives her name in turn. At the end of the dance, if they have not been cut-in on, the boy then takes her to a seat, or he may ask her if she is free for the following dance.

In some communities, however, it is the custom for a girl to dance only with her date. When you are where that rule prevails, stick to it. You'll always find that you get along better and are better liked if you abide by the standard procedure.

Many of us wonder what to do if we are stuck. A girl, who finds that she has been dancing with one boy for what seems an interminable length of time,

can always beg to be excused and make tracks for the powder room. But a boy who is in the same predicament has no alternative but to keep on dancing until the music stops, at which time he can take the girl back to her chair.

It is an escort's responsibility to keep an eye on his date — to see to it that she does not get stuck or that she is not suddenly left flat in the middle of the dance floor.

It is not necessary to keep up a steady stream of chatter while dancing. Lots of people, in fact, like some silence now and then so that they can concentrate on the music. Others prefer to break up the silence with a few comments, a remark on the orchestra, or an observation about the decorations, etc. You have only to fit yourself to the mood of your partner. Don't be afraid of holding your peace.

Should you get a partner who dances badly, don't let him feel that you are annoyed. Poor boy, he is no doubt very aware of his clumsiness, so try to put him at his ease. If he is really dreadful, and obviously uncomfortable, you can suggest sitting this one out, or indicate that you would love to stop for refreshments. Should it be you who commits the offense of stepping on *his* toes, apologize sweetly but not too often. If you dance very badly, take lessons. A girl who must constantly excuse herself for treading on her partner's toes will not be asked to dance often. Boys are pretty fussy about such things. Though they may dance badly themselves, they expect a girl to dance well. It may be unfair, but it's true.

Be careful about what you say to your dance partners. Personal comments are not in order. You may think you are being witty when you criticize another's dress, or hold up to ridicule another's hair-do, but you'll get your rightful comeuppance when you find out that you've been jeering at your partner's date or his sister. Besides, a boy may think — and rightly so — that a girl who's so ready with criticism will get in a few licks about *him* the moment he's turned the corner.

Flamboyant behavior of any kind is bad manners on a dance floor. Loud talk, boisterous bouncing, or flinging about of arms and legs is neither pretty to see nor polite.

When a girl has finished dancing with a partner she should smile and let him know how much she has enjoyed it (whether she has or hasn't). The boy is expected to say, "Thank you."

If you are attending a private dance, given by one hostess or a group of hostesses, you should on leave-taking thank them for the good time you have had. Should the hostess retire before the end of the evening, you should take the opportunity at that time for expressing your appreciation of the fun provided.

After the last dance, when the party has broken up, the girl and her escort go to search out their belongings and upon meeting again make their way homeward. A boy is responsible for seeing his date to her door, unless some other arrangement has been made with her parents beforehand. Perhaps her family have said they will come to pick her up. He, however, should not leave her side until she is delivered into the safekeeping of her family.

It need not be said, I trust, that chaperones should receive the attention and respect of all the young guests. They should not be tricked or made fun of. They are there to see to it that the dance runs smoothly and properly. Many of them would, perhaps, much prefer to be home in bed. Don't make their evening a constant trial.

At a dance away from home — a college prom, for instance — you are expected to do much as you would at home. The rules are the same, save that instead of being returned to your home you are returned to your quarters for the weekend. You must abide by any regulations which the colleges have established and do so graciously and willingly. Don't make things difficult for your date by trying to outsmart the authorities. You will only get the two of you in trouble.

On saying good-night to your date, tell him what fun you've had. Make him feel that you've really, truly enjoyed yourself. He has gone to a lot of trouble and expense to see to it that you had fun. Let him know you're appreciative.

Young girls should remember to carry

in their purses enough money to take care of the tip for the attendant in the powder room. How much you give depends on the services you have received. Don't forget that if you suddenly find yourself coming undone, a hem ravelling, a strap broken, you can always go to the attendant for a repair job. Many powder rooms are also equipped with emergency supplies, such as band-aids, aspirins, etc.

If a boy has taken the girl's coat to be checked, it is he who will be responsible for picking it up again and for the tipping. If, however, the girl checks her things herself (this is often true where the check room and powder room are adjacent), then it is she who will pick up her own things and do the necessary tipping.

A wise precaution for any girl is to have with her enough cash to cover emergencies, so-called "mad money." One never knows what will come up in the course of an evening and it is better to be prepared.

To Remember

1. Be dressed and ready on time.
2. Accept your corsage (if given) graciously and with sincerity.
3. Your first and last dances are reserved for your date.
4. Don't be such a belle of the ball that you have no time for your date.
5. Never make an exhibition of yourself when dancing.
6. Carry enough money to take care of emergencies, and your share of tipping.

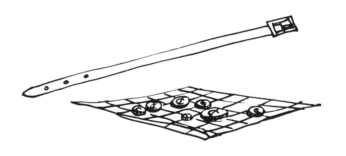

16

Be a Hostess

Being a hostess is being yourself. You change not a whit of your personality. Some people think that they have got to go through some mysterious transformation in order to give a party or have a friend for the weekend. 'Tain't so. All you have to do is act naturally, but with responsibility.

Responsibility is the secret of any hostess' success. By that I mean thinking ahead and planning. A party just doesn't run itself. It has to have refreshments and some sort of general scheme. And it has to have people. So first off are the invitations.

Whether you mail or telephone them, invitations should be sent out to everyone you wish to include. A point to remember here is to be generous. Don't boycott friends you happen to be peeved with. Don't keep your list down to just the same old circle. Vary your guests.

Be prepared before the guests arrive. Have your refreshments ready (for ideas see page 112), and the living room or game room spic and span. If you intend to play records, see to it that the machine is in working order and that a selection of music is available. Clear the floor for dancing.

As your guests come in, greet each one and show them where to leave their hats and coats. Be glad to see each new arrival and make everyone feel at home. Nothing is grimmer than to arrive at a party and feel as if your hostess had wished you'd stayed at home.

If as the party progresses, accidents happen (and they sometimes do), be efficient but gracious about cleaning up the wreckage. Never let a guest who's broken a glass or spilled punch on the floor feel your wrath. The offender knows he's been clumsy and is suffering the tortures of the damned, so do all you can to put him at his ease. Laugh off as much as you can, but own up to any damage to your parents. It's their house that's taking the beating.

To avoid wreckage, keep a good grip on your party. Without ever being a wet blanket you can hold down those extra-boisterous spirits who want to play football with your mother's best lamp. One of the best ways to stop any nonsense is to see to it that one or both of your parents drop in on the merriment from time to time.

As each guest departs, you see him to the door. Be sure that he has all he came with — hat, coat and gloves — and turn on the hall lights so that he doesn't stumble around in the dark. With your mother's help you should arrange that all the girls have a way home, so that none of them has to be out alone at night. Usually the situation clears itself up, as your guests arrive two by two and depart the same way. But transportation is something that a good hostess doesn't overlook.

A well run party can never be achieved without some help from your mother. Take her advice to heart and do as she asks you. If she sets an hour for a departure deadline, don't wail and scream, but see to it that your guests understand that a time limit has been set. Such precautions are always made for your own good.

Sometime you may want to give a party — say a luncheon party — that takes place in a restaurant and not in your own house. Such a party certainly takes a lot of strain off mother and the kitchen, but

it doesn't relieve you of any responsibility. You've still got your job to do to see to it that all your guests have a good time.

As hostess you should arrive at the restaurant or club or wherever you are meeting well ahead of time in order to be on hand to greet your friends as they come in. If possible, reserve your table ahead of time. When everyone has gathered, you can then be seated without having to mill around waiting for a table to be free.

If there is a headwaiter, you give him your name and tell him that you have reserved a table, and you follow him to wherever your place may be. If there is no one to show the way, you should be the first in line, so that you can show your guests the way.

Once settled, and menu in hand, ask each girl what she would like to order. Make a few suggestions so that no one feels shy about requesting this or that. When the waiter is ready to take the orders, you are the one to tell him what's what. You are the one, too, who keeps an eye out to see that water glasses are kept filled and everyone has just what she ordered.

If there is a guest of honor, it is thoughtful to have a "little something" for her, a flower or pretty boutonniere. She should be made to feel festive, and you should do all you can to let her know this is her day.

Keep conversation general and don't let anyone (including yourself) run away with a monologue.

When the time comes to pay the check, do it quietly and without ostentation. Don't brag about the size of the bill. How much you paid for your party should be a secret between you and the management. Sometimes you will find it convenient to have the check charged to your parents' account; some restaurants and almost all clubs permit this. It makes the money part much easier to handle, and keeps it utterly secret, since all you have to do is sign your name to the check. But be sure that the head-waiter knows who you are. You can also include the tip in the check by adding the amount you want to tip to the amount of the meal, labelling it "tip." Tip twelve to fifteen percent of the total amount.

If it is possible for you to arrange the menu in advance, do so by all means; it saves the time, the fuss and the confusion that individual ordering takes. You can also know who your waiter is to be, tip him in advance, and even arrange to pay in advance. Such planning makes your guests think that you have actually put as much time and effort into entertaining them as if you were having them in your own house.

As you get up to go — and you start the procession — look around to see that nobody has forgotten anything. Keep a smiling face until your guests have gone their separate ways; then go ahead and heave a sigh if you feel like it.

It's not always necessary to assume the full responsibility of being a hostess. You can give parties where everybody pitches in. Round up a picnic where each guest contributes something — a hard boiled egg here, a buttered roll there. Think about a platter party where you provide the vic, the guests bring the records. There are all kinds of twists.

Not all parties need to be given just for fun. You can plan productive parties. Perhaps you may want to organize a group to help out on a Red Cross or a church project. Everybody shares the work. All you have to do is to be a headquarters. Refreshments can be limited to a coke, pretzels and potato chips, or milk and cookies.

One of the most important things about being a good hostess is to be prepared for emergencies. If someone calls up at the last minute and says he can't come, don't wilt and weep like a willow. If an extra girl turns up, a friend of a friend of a friend, don't push her out the door. Make plans, yes, but be elastic about them. Things that get too cut and dried taste stale.

A girl who is a good hostess has learned to do well something that lots of us dread

— making introductions. Why introductions are such a terror I've never been able to figure out, but they certainly stumped me for a time. I was the kind of girl who could hardly remember her own name when faced with having to say: "Mother, this is —," or "Father, I'd like you to meet —."

I've found out that it takes some of the terror out of introductions if you think of them as the only possible way two people who have never seen each other before can get acquainted. When you understand what an introduction does, instead of getting all twisted up in the formulas, it helps a lot.

I figured out one day what would happen if you just left two strangers staring at each other without someone saying, "My name is so and so," and the prospects were so dreadful that I haven't worried about introductions since. I've realized that in spite of all the rules and regulations, introducing and being introduced is lots easier than just standing in dismal silence.

To show just how introductions work and what is involved I am going to make up a few examples. If some of them seem complicated to you, take time out to think how much simpler it is to do it this way than to flounder around without names or guideposts of any kind.

Let's start out by pretending that you have a cousin named Ann Smith. She has come to visit you for the first time. She has never met any of your friends and in fact doesn't know a single soul in town. Now, it's obvious that if Ann is not introduced to at least a few people, she is not going to have much fun, nor is she going to feel very welcome. After all, sightseeing goes just so far. What makes a visit interesting is the new friends and new faces that you meet.

O.K. Here's Ann on the one hand, you on the other, and together you go into the drug store. Sitting at the counter are a group of your best chums. What do you do? Very simple. You say to the assembled crew: "Hi! I'd like you to meet my cousin Ann Smith, who is staying with me. Ann, meet the gang." And then you go around the circle naming names. Ann won't remember them all, but at least she will feel that the ice has been broken.

Now let's pretend that you give a party in Ann's honor. At the appointed time you and Ann are waiting, all set, for the door bell to ring. What is easier than to say to each newcomer: "Hello so and so. So glad you could come. I want you to meet my cousin Ann Smith, who is staying with me." Then you turn to Ann and say: "Ann, this is Mary Jones (or Susis Smith or whoever it may be)." No trick to it at all, is there?

Continuing with Ann (such a convenient cousin!), let's suppose that you and she are walking down the street. You see a friend and stop to chat. Ann may walk on a little, if you are only going to be a minute, but if your conversation begins to drag out, it's up to you to call Ann back and introduce her. Otherwise Ann is going to feel mighty awkward if she has to gaze at a shop window for agonizing minutes on end while you gossip on and on.

Still with me? Do you see that the whole point of an introduction is to make things easier and more pleasant for a stranger, to give her a sense of belonging, of knowing people? Fine, because now we are going on to a new problem. This time we are pretending that the out-of-town cousin is a boy. His name is Charles Brown. There is very little difference between your handling of Charles and your handling of Ann, except that since Charles is a boy, you must remember that he is introduced *to* your girl friends. Men are always presented to women, because it is supposed that women, as the gentler sex, are the ones to whom deference is due. For that reason you say the girl's name first and Charles' afterwards. Like this: "Mary, this is my cousin Charles Brown from Milwaukee. Charles, this is Mary Jones, one of my best friends."

So long as you are dealing with people of your own age, you never have to worry who takes precedence over whom. Everybody is equal. It makes little difference who gets named first in your introductions of girls to girls, boys to boys. It is only when you have to introduce a boy to a girl that you must remember to put the girl first. However, when you are involved with older people, you should keep in mind that respect for age counts a great deal. It is just common decency to show your elders some deference if only for the reason that they have lived longer than you. That is why younger people are always introduced *to* older ones, and why a young person should always rise to meet an older person and remain standing until invited to sit down.

Let's take an example. You bring home a girl friend from school. When you arrive at your door, all that you need say is this: "Mother (the first person named is the person to whom you make the presentation), this is Mary Jones, who is in my class at school. Mary, my mother." That's all. Not so painful as some of us make it out to be. Note that Mary, if she has good manners, waits to see if your mother puts out her hand — it's up to the older person to make the gesture. If your mother chooses to do so, Mary takes it and says graciously, "How do you do." Don't say, "Pleased-to-meet-cha," a phrase that has been so thoroughly overdone that it no longer means anything. Do, when you shake hands, give a good firm shake — a cold fish of a shake makes a bad impression. So does an over-long pump-handle motion.

Now, let's suppose that instead of your mother, you find your father at home. You are wondering what to do, for on one hand I have told you that ladies are presented to gentlemen and on the other that younger people are presented to their elders. In science, when two forces meet head on, one's got to give way. So, too, in society. In this case, age gives way to youth. Courtesy gives top billing to the ladies — and how nice that, in spite of modern career equality, the gentler sex still gets a few licks in. So, put pa last in the phrasing of your introduction: "Mary, this is my father. Daddy, Mary Jones."

If we want to get complicated, we can suppose all kinds of situations. Here is one. You have the whole gang over at your house for the afternoon when your mother suddenly enters the room. Everybody gets up, of course; that's the first thing, for young people always rise for their elders. Then it's your turn to take over. You say: "Mother, I don't think you know everybody here," and you go about the room introducing your friends in order.

Both parents will be mighty proud of you when you handle all these situations with ease. Remember that they want you to have poise and they'll do everything they can to help. Don't turn your back on their aid. Perhaps you'll find that they are more than willing to practice with you at home so that you can get the feeling of the thing. Assurance comes from having more than a nodding acquaintance with a subject and it is as true of introductions as it is of the history of ancient Greece. When you really know what you're about, you'll never feel flustered or embarrassed. You won't duck side streets for fear of having to introduce a new teacher to your mother, or a school pal to your father. ·

You won't be called on often to introduce older people to each other. However, if and when you do find yourself in this situation, go about it with the same easy fluency that you have with your own friends. Don't get stilted and pompous. Just remember, gentlemen are presented to ladies. Keep in mind precedence of dignity, age and position. There's a knack to knowing what are the subtle shadings, but you are not expected to be up on all of that. If you make a mistake, don't let it throw you. Better to have tried than to have got all red in the face and not tried at all.

No doubt you will be comforted to learn that there are occasions when introductions are not necessary. For example, it is not necessary to introduce everybody at a party, for the mere fact that people are all collected under one roof is supposed to dispense with the need. Two strangers can perfectly well start up a conversation, introducing themselves to each other without having to wait for a third person to come along to do the honors. Just say, if you find yourself in a corner with someone you don't know, "My name is —" and begin to chat. Don't let shyness hold you back. If you prefer, you don't have to begin with your name. You can simply talk. Later on you can exchange names, if you wish, or you can simply let the matter of identity drop.

Remember that once you have been introduced to someone, you can then greet him the next time you meet. When

walking down the street, nod and smile. In a gathering say: "Hello, nice to see you again." Should you discover that the person you are greeting doesn't seem to remember you, don't get flustered. Many people have a bad memory for names and faces. It doesn't mean that they are trying to give you a cold shoulder. They simply don't remember you. Take it in your stride. If you are reintroduced and the person can't recall that this all happened before, don't call it to his attention. You may make him feel stupid and clumsy.

You can always make it easier for people to remember introductions if you pronounce names clearly and if you tack on a little something to identify the person. For instance, in introducing somebody to your cousin Ann (dear old Ann, back with us again), you can say, "Ann, this is Mary Jones, who just won the tennis championship." That helps to place Mary in Ann's memory as a tennis player and also gives Ann something to talk about with Mary, a subject with which to begin a conversation. It always makes things easier for people if they have been given a fact to cling to when they start to talk together for the first time.

Should you find yourself in the position of not being able to remember a person's name and you know that you've met before, be honest about it. Lots of people have had that dreadful sinking sensation that they've seen the face before, but oh, what is the name! There's nothing to do but say, "I'm awfully sorry but I can't remember your name." Better to own up than to mumble something unintelligible. You may have to make an introduction to a third person, and then you'll give yourself away for sure and seem foolish in the process. But don't worry if it happens to you. It's not a tragedy.

The same thing holds true when you've been introduced to someone whose name you did not catch. If you, in turn, are called upon to introduce the stranger again to a third person, own up that you did not catch the name. Then when the name has been repeated, make sure that you say it clearly for the benefit of the newcomer. You'll be blessed for your courtesy. There are so few people who really try to say a name clearly that the few who do are adored for their efforts. You will win the undying affection of all those souls who usually hear themselves introduced as Joe or Jane Mumble-Mumble.

This seems as good a time as any to mention *house guests*. Having friends stay with you is an acid test of your powers of hostessing. Always remember that anyone who visits you, for a night or a month, has left the comfort of her own home to put up with yours. Therefore show you appreciate the sacrifice by taking some pains about her coming.

Be sure that her room is in applepie order. If she shares your room, clean out a bureau drawer or two, and put extra hangers in the closet. Tell her the hours for all meals and dates. Nothing's worse for a guest's nerves than lying in bed wondering whether she's hours early or late for breakfast. At night it's up to you or your parents to suggest going to bed.

She will be forever grateful to you if before she has to meet your gang you tip her off on local cutsoms, taboos, sore subjects, surefire hits. Above all, don't worry about whether your friends will like her. If they're real friends they'll give her a whirl. She'll have a whale of a time and so will you.

To Remember

1. Introduce a younger person to an older one, an inferior to a superior (such as an Ensign to an Admiral.)
2. A gentleman is always introduced to a lady.
3. Younger people rise for older people; a gentleman for a lady.
4. Many persons judge people by their hand shake; how's yours? Like a dead fish? When shaking hands, give a firm grasp — let the person feel you're interested in meeting him.
5. Young people remain standing throughout an introduction and do not sit until invited to do so.
6. Names should be pronounced clearly during an introduction. It is helpful to add a descriptive phrase to fix the person in the memory, and to give a nudge to conversation.

17

Away From Home

Whether it's for an hour or two, a day or two, a week or two, the time you spend away from home is time well spent in having fun. So much goes on outside the house in the way of parties, dances, club meetings, weekends and vacations that it's often hard to cram them all in.

To enjoy your activities off home base to their fullest there are a few things you ought to keep in mind. The most important is that you be cooperative. If the gang wants to play charades and you'd rather dance, for Heaven's sake go along with the group. When you're staying overnight with Sally, do just as Sally's mother wants you to do. Don't ever say, "But at home I don't have to drink milk with dinner," etc.

You know the kind of cooperation I mean. It's a spirit of willingness and good humor that makes you fun to have around. It's a point of view that remains constant whether you are enjoying yourself or are so bored that you keep wishing you could disappear in a puff of smoke.

A cooperative person asks to help set the table, wash dishes, clean up and put away when she's having dinner with a friend. She doesn't wait to be asked, but anticipates a need. She also makes her own bed, leaves the bathroom neat and tidy and keeps all her possessions together. She's the kind of girl that people love to have visit, who's never any trouble because she doesn't make any trouble.

No matter how hard you try, there are bound to be times when things go wrong. If the catastrophe is an honest accident, don't brood about it. Accidents can happen to anyone. I remember a party at Prentice-Hall (they publish my books, you know) when I dropped a glass. I can't tell you to this day how it happened, but one minute it was in my hand, and the next it was a big puddle on the floor. I had tried so hard to make a good impression and suddenly there I stood, feeling all thumbs. I was certain that everybody in the room was staring at me and thinking, "What a dumb, clumsy girl." However, when I woke up enough to look around I realized that nobody was paying any attention. A waiter came and cleaned up the mess, I apologized, and the incident was over.

Another time I was at a party given at my friend Carole's house. I broke the crystal punch ladle — a blow to end all blows. Of course I apologized, but I did more than that. The next morning I wrote a note of apology and I also replaced the ladle. I was lucky in that I was able to match the pattern. Sometimes things that you break turn out to be irreplaceable. When you go through the seat of an antique chair or overturn an 18th century Chinese porcelain lamp, there's nothing you can do in the way of replacement. All you can hope to do is to show that you are genuinely sorry, and pray that you are not black-listed forever. Most people, fortunately, realize that accidents such as these can and do happen, and that no precious possession is safe except locked in storage or under glass in a museum. Still, the fact that breakage does occur and that people gradually accustom themselves to loss should not make us any the less wary about our actions. You'll find that if you keep your movements in control, your feet in balance and your eyes in front of you, your accident ratio will be small.

One of the reasons parents frown on wild parties is that they know by experience that someone or something sooner or later is going to come to a sorry end. Broken china and bashed chins too often are the result of touch football practiced indoors.

Responsibility — oh, how that word keeps cropping up! — is what makes or breaks a visitor's reputation. The responsibility to be self-sufficient, to be useful, to be pleasant and good-natured (even at the beach after forty-eight hours of rain), to be enthusiastic and attractive.

One of the first responsibilities of a guest in the house, whether for twenty-four hours or two weeks, is to fit in with the house's schedule. If everybody in the family gets up for breakfast, don't expect yours in bed. If everybody goes to church on Sunday, don't ask to play tennis. If your hosts disapprove of late hours, don't get your friend in Dutch by demanding to stay out till two in the morning.

A second responsibility of the guest in the house is being prompt. If you have agreed to arrive on the 5:15 train, arrive on that train. Unless a drastic misadventure has waylaid you, don't expect to have your hosts greet you with calm countenances if you show up on the 10:02. Companion to the arriving on time is departing on time. If you say that you are leaving Sunday evening, leave then. Weekend guests who stay over until the middle of the next week are as welcome as a rainstorm on a picnic.

There are good reasons why the responsible guest is appreciated. First off, a hostess can make plans and know that they will stick. She knows when to meet a train, how much food to have in the house, what to plan as recreation — a swim, a sail, a game of tennis, and she also knows that, the good Lord willing, these carefully plotted plans will come to pass.

Secondly, a girl who keeps her room in order, is meticulous about cleanliness, is willing and able to help out, not only at the outdoor barbecue, but indoors as well, does not make extra chores for the household. In this day and age of servantless houses, few people can afford to put up guests who demand service. Everybody's got to pitch in.

Third, a young person who is responsible makes a hostess feel comfortable. After all, your hostess is concerned for your well-being. She has to answer to your mother should anything go wrong; that's why she breathes more easily if she can see right off that you are not the kind who is going to leap off tree tops or dash out into the night to look at the moon and be one with nature.

No matter where you go, these rules of responsibility hold true. Best behavior, fit for maiden aunts and ministers, is what you should always put forward. This goes for college weekends and house parties too. I grant, of course, that a fraternity dance is somewhat more relaxed than tea with Great-aunt Cecelia, but the basic tenets remain the same. Sincerity, honesty, and good taste are in. Loud talk and kittenish cut-ups are out.

Let's take a college weekend from start to finish as a good example of what is expected of a poised young woman — You. It all begins with an invitation — a letter, a telephone call, a personal appeal. You're in the skies, but you better keep two feet on earth.

After you've mentally accepted the invitation — and, silly girl, what other answer than yes is there to a bid from a college man? — you talk to your parents to get their permission. If you are away at school yourself, you go through the prescribed steps to get permission from

the school authorities. Well armed with all the necessary papers, you give the nod to your date.

Between yourselves you work out your plan of arrival. You agree to meet at the station at the such and such train. Now make certain you are reading the right time table, so you won't find yourself stranded twenty miles from civilization with only your luggage to keep you company.

Luggage reminds me that it is important to pack everything you need. Elsewhere I have talked about the importance of having the right kind of clothes for the right occasion. All I want to mention here is that you should not forget the evening dress, if there is to be a dance, or shorts and shirt if there is to be a picnic. College weekend clothes are pretty standard fare. You won't go wrong if you take just what all your friends are taking. When you're young it's better to look like everybody else than to be an individualist. College men are conservative. They run from razzle-dazzle except on the football field.

Lesson one in "How to Handle College Men" is: college men are conservatives. They like their women to be pretty, but not movie queens; to be intelligent, but not Quiz Kids; peppy, but not persistent. In other words, a college man wants a well-rounded girl who knows what the score is.

Having met your man of the hour — or of the next forty-eight, you'll find that the next step is to get yourself settled in your quarters. He will have made the arrangements, and you take what you get. Usually you'll be sharing your room with lots of other dates and you'll be under the supervision of an adult. If you are to stay at a hotel, it is bound to be one that is approved by the college and which abides by college rules and regulations.

Lesson number two in "How to Handle, etc.," is to realize that certain rules and regulations set up by college authorities exist and you are to act accordingly. Don't try to wiggle out. It's not smart and it can be dangerous.

Once settled and having combed your hair, you'll usually find that for the rest of the weekend you have hardly time to draw a breath. Games, parties, dances every minute. A big whirl. You won't be bothered by any of it, if you act naturally and keep your head. Don't get carried away by the excitement and do things that you would never dream of doing at your high school prom. For instance, don't disappear with another boy. Don't ask your date for special favors. Follow along with the gang and keep in step. A college weekend is just like any other weekend at home except that it is probably more fun because more things are happening. Keep in the uproar and you'll find that what you may have feared — the crowds, the constant change of pace — will all fall in line. You'll have the time of your life! You'll probably tell your grandchildren all about it — what fun it was at your first college prom.

18

The Mail In Your Life

I like to get letters. Most people do. It's nice to have something other than the funny papers to read. Still, to get letters, you must write letters, and that's where the system sometimes breaks down. There are people who want all the fun and no work. They complain that they can't write because they haven't anything to say. Cornered at a desk, they are more than likely to begin: "Nothing happening here. Life is very dull."

The truth of the matter is that there is always something happening everywhere. Remember that the people to whom you write are not on the spot; therefore *anything* that has occurred is

of interest to them. To you the football game played last weekend, Sunday's picnic, are all done and over, but they are still fresh and alive to your readers who have not yet heard about them. So put down the details. Tell all you can. Make your letter worth its three cent stamp.

When you are writing a letter don't fuss over minor do-thises-do-thats. Don't stew so long about not beginning the first sentence with *I* that you never begin at all. Plunge into your news — your sister had her hair cut — the dance at the Club was a huge success — you are considering taking a summer job — etc. When you come to the end of the news, STOP.

Don't feel compelled to go on to the bottom of the page. Don't try to find an excuse to close. Just stop. Add your best wishes, remember yourself to friends and family, send your love, then sign your name.

The letter that I have attempted to describe above is the kind of chatty letter that you exchange with friends. It is the everyday sort of letter that you receive and answer in kind. Not all letters fall into this category. There are letters of congratulation, of thanks, of condolence, of acceptance, of business. Each one has a special form and a special significance.

Let's start off with the formal letter of acceptance. To begin with, it is not so much a letter as it is a formula. Written to answer a formal invitation, it follows a cut and dried pattern in which there is no room allowed for individual or personal touches. It is written in the third person form of the invitation, on conservative note paper, is well spaced on the page, and paraphrases precisely the wording of the invitation. Examples:

> Miss Betty Cornell
> accepts with pleasure
> (or, regrets that owing to a previous engagement she is unable to accept)
> Mr. and Mrs. Charles Smith's
> kind invitation
> to the reception following
> the wedding of their daughter
> Mary Agnes
> August the fourth

Always be careful when answering an invitation which requires a formal answer (and you'll know a written answer, whether yes or no, is required when you see "R.S.V.P." written in the corner of the card) to write in blue ink in your best penmanship. A formal acceptance is not the place for fancy touches, for cute note paper, for colored inks.

In writing a letter or note of acceptance to an invitation which is not couched along the prescribed formal lines, you have room for some individual thinking. However, don't overstep. Stay within bounds and keep your answer to the point.

For instance:

Dear Mrs. Smith:

Thank you so much for your kind invitation to spend a weekend in the country. I would love to come and I am looking forward to getting a good tan after spending so much of my summer in the city. I will arrive on Friday, on the 5:15 train, as you suggested.

Mother joins me in sending you our best regards.

> Sincerely yours,
> August 28, 19— *Betty Cornell*

Such a letter tries to be gracious, without being long-winded. It is written on note paper, in ink, and is spaced neatly on the page. It should be dated and should contain all pertinent information — such as arrival time. Any questions asked in the original invitation should be answered. Please be sure that your spelling is correct and that your handwriting is legible. Such things make a great deal of difference in the impression that you make on people, particularly older people. Failure to take pains is often rightly considered a breach of courtesy because it is assumed that you did not care enough to do your best job.

Now let's turn to letters of congratulation. These are somewhat like the note described above, informal, but not uninhibited. They should be enthusiastic but brief.

Here's an example of what you might say to a college friend of your brother's, a boy you know slightly.

Dear John,

How excited I am to learn that you have been elected President of the class. I think it is wonderful and an honor you certainly deserve.

All my best wishes for lots of success in your year of office,

Sincerely,

November 11, 19—   *Betty*

Here's a suggestion for a note to a girl who has recently become engaged:

Dear Mary,

Really, I can't tell you how delighted we all are to hear of your engagement to Jim Brown. He is just the nicest husband anyone could have. Of course you deserve only the best.

We do hope you'll both come and see us soon so we can all celebrate.

Affectionately,

Betty

Or, a letter to a school friend in bed with a broken leg:

Dear Mary,

How sorry I am to hear about your accident! I hope that you are feeling better now and that you'll soon be up and about. We are planning all sorts of good times as soon as you are able to join us. We miss you at school — English class just isn't the same.

Love,

Betty

Much the nicest kind of letter to write (from your point of view) is that of thanks, for it indicates by its very nature that you have just received a gift. Whether the gift be one of a weekend, a service rendered, or a present wrapped in tissue paper and ribbon, you must never neglect to say "Thank you." A thank-you note should be written as soon as possible after the event. Don't put it off.

Dear Grandmother,

What a perfectly beautiful scarf! You can't imagine how much I love it. The color is beautiful and it matches exactly my winter coat. You are a dear to think of me every birthday in such wonderful ways.

With all my very best love to you and to Grandfather,

Affectionately,

Betty

or —

Dear Mrs. Smith:

Thank you ever so much for the wonderful weekend in the country. I don't know when I've had such a good time. You were always kind and thoughtful. Mother says you are the finest hostess she knows and I certainly agree with her.

Sincerely yours,

Betty

I trust that I have made it clear that all these notes should be written on note paper in ink. Typing is out — except for letters to very close friends, and then only when you are writing casually. Notes are handwritten and must be neat. No blotches, no erasures, no scratchings out.

The same thing goes for the envelopes, which should have the address carefully placed on the envelope and well spaced. The stamp, as you know, goes right side up in the upper right corner.

When it comes to business letters, the rules of neatness hold more than ever true. These letters you may type, indeed should type if you know how, so that they will be easy to read, easy to file. The address of the firm goes on the left hand side of the page above the salutation. Like this:

August 30, 19—

Smith and Co.
100 Main St.
New York, N. Y.

Dear Sirs:

The black patent leather hatbox which I ordered on August 15 arrived today. Unfortunately, however, the handle was broken and the leather torn. I am returning it to you under separate cover. Please replace it with a duplicate in perfect condition.

Very truly yours,
Betty Cornell
685 Linden Ave.
Teaneck, N. J.

Note: The address of the business firm and the address of the letter writer are always given. The first at the top of the page; the second at the bottom, below the signature.

Some of the most important letters in your life will be the letters you have the sense not to write, or if you write, that you have the sense not to mail. I am, of course, talking about the gooey love letter or the nasty note of anger. All letters, in fact, in which you let go both barrels, are liable to catch you up some day, make you squirm to think that you ever exposed your private thoughts in black and white.

If you have something on your chest that you feel you've got to say or burst, go ahead and put it down on paper, but don't mail it! Burn it up! Remember that a letter once in the mailbox is out of your hands. You can't correct it, change a word, alter the meaning. You've done the deed and there's no back-tracking. So, beware!

Beware also of writing that dreamy boy you met at the beach last summer before he writes you. He may have said

that he loved you truly, but if weeks have gone by and there's no word from him, no postcard, no nothing, don't pour out your soul on paper. You can write him a chatty note and hope for the best, but if it goes unanswered, you can only grit your teeth and bear it. It won't do any good to pelt him with mail. You don't wear your heart on your sleeve with the boys at home, so why expose the poor palpitating thing in the futile guise of air mail and special delivery stickers to the boys away from home?

Last of all I want to remind you that letters are still, in spite of telegraphs and telephones, one of the most pleasant things in life. They give you a chance to share with another person, in quiet and leisure, your ideas, your plans, your present moment. They are worth far more than the cost of paper, ink and stamp. They are part of you.

To Remember

1. Always write legibly, neatly and clearly.
2. Type only business or chatty personal notes. Otherwise use pen and ink. Take care to suit your paper to your purpose.
3. Address envelopes carefully. Glue the stamp neatly. Put return address in upper left hand corner.
4. Answer promptly.
5. Thank-you notes are an immediate must.

19

Helpful Hints—'Tis Better to Give

That old saw about giving being better than receiving is not far wrong. You really do get more pleasure out of giving someone else a present than you do in getting one yourself. No matter how much or how little you spend on a gift, if you have taken time and trouble to select the very thing that will hit the spot, you get a kick out of it.

It has been said before, but it bears saying again, money has nothing to do with the value of a gift. The pair of socks you knit yourself means more to your father or to your best beau than the most expensive gold-cornered crocodile wallet you could buy. A sachet of dried roses, cut from the garden, will delight Mother more than all the most expensive lingerie in the world.

It's nice, I know, to have the feeling when gift-giving time comes around that you have enough money to buy all the things you want, but that feeling doesn't often occur. Most of us are as broke as can be. It's not necessary, however, to let yourself get despondent and cranky over cash. There are many gifts that cost almost nothing, yet are sure to bring pleasure. Often these are things you can make yourself — not only clothes, but food (how about a cake for the next family birthday!), and knick-knacks like a felt eyeglass case for Mother's glasses (maybe decorated with sequins), or shoe bags for your father if he travels a lot.

There are times, too, when an expensive gift is out of place. You should never make a lavish display for a boy, no matter how fond you are of him. It is in bad taste to spend a fortune on any young man. No matter what the occasion — birthday, Christmas, graduation — keep your gift small, a gesture, a memento. Making argyle socks is one of the best things I can think of. Other suggestions are wallets, key chains, books, records; but never, never, solid gold cuff links.

Special occasion gifts often take the form of graduation presents, baby presents, confirmation presents. For graduation or confirmation, you can get sentimental — for a girl friend, perhaps a charm for a bracelet marked with the date; for a boy, perhaps a key ring marked with the date. From your own family you may expect a watch or a ring, but these you never give.

Babies are fun. Since they are so new, there is lots you can find for them. Baby clothes, blankets, sweaters, socks, and, on a more expensive level, silver drinking cups and spoons. Often you know from the mother something she'd like to have. Other times you can find out from a mutual friend.

By now you can see there is a real technique to good gift-giving. It takes thought and preparation (and in many instances advance leg work, like finding out sizes and color preferences) but it pays off in genuine enjoyment and heart-felt thanks.

You can make a well chosen gift even more welcome if you wrap it prettily. People love to open a beautiful package. Indeed, in Japan the way a package is wrapped is as important as what is inside. There the wrappings are meant to be admired as well as the gift; and a donor is hurt if she is not complimented on the beauty of her wrapping. Here we do not go to such extremes, but it is true that a pretty package does make a

gift seem more personal, more gala. Do take time to wrap your gift well — choose papers that go with the season, tie ribbons daintily, write your card neatly.

Don't forget that as a weekend guest you should have a gift for your hostess. It need not be much, a box of candy or a few flowers. It is given as an expression of your appreciation of hospitality and should be presented with that idea in mind.

So often we look on gifts that we give as a chore, a vicious "she gave me, so I gave her." Don't let that be your case. Gift-giving — especially spontaneous gift-giving — a present for no reason at all — can be fun. When you get in the spirit, you'll find it true that it is better to give than to receive. Beyond the usual occasions for exchanging gifts you'd be surprised the number of times you'll give something just because you want to — a scarf to Janie, your best friend, because you know she's wanted one; a bouquet of flowers to your mother just to say you love her.

When it is your turn to receive, you know the pleasure you feel from the spontaneous gift — how suddenly bright the whole world looks because someone has sent you a surprise present.

Granted that most of the gifts you get are not surprises, still it is fun to get them just the same. But did you, because you knew in advance that your Christmas present was to be a charm bracelet, fail to express your thanks when it is finally unwrapped? Some of us tend to get a little blasé sometimes. We know that every year there will be presents from the family, from Aunt Mary, from Joe. We begin to expect them and instead of being over-joyed to have them, we start to take an almost critical attitude toward the haul.

Worst of all, if the present turns out to be something you'd never want to own in a month of Sundays, you assume a really sour attitude. Let's not forget to be grateful for what we get. Most of the time it is something wonderful to have, so let's tell the donor about it — let him know how truly appreciative we are. Go ahead and fling your arms around your father and tell him that string of beads is just exactly what you'd been hoping for.

Grudging thanks are bad manners. It takes very little to be enthusiastic about a gift — and it hurts so many feelings when you aren't. No excuses can undo the damage. Certainly, the cardinal rule of good manners is that you should never injure another person, and often that's just what we tend to do. We put off writing thank-you notes. We don't tell Mother how much we loved the new dress, we just hang it in the closet. We accept Jane's birthday compact with a "thanks very much," said in an off-hand kind of way.

There is such a thing as being stickily over-sweet and gushy, but there is no such thing as being over-genuinely enthusiastic and pleased. Sincere pleasure, nicely expressed, is all that anyone wants. Too bad they seldom get it.

A generous person who gives easily can often get involved in a merry-go-round of borrowing and lending. The wisest policy, of course, is to "neither a borrower nor a lender be." That way you will never be subject to recriminations, loss of property, unpleasant scenes. Certainly if you must be one or the other, be a lender rather than a borrower.

The difficulty about borrowing is that few people take a responsible attitude toward another's property. Should you ever get in the position where you must borrow something, do remember to be careful, extra careful. Seldom can an object be replaced — never, if it has sentimental value. Value of any sort is a touchy thing to describe. Perhaps Jane's evening dress, worn three times, has not much real (money) value, but it means a lot to Jane because it suits her more than any other. You borrowed it, tore it and now it's useless. You can, and should, offer to pay for another, but not even a new dress can be to Jane what the other was.

Sometimes borrowing gets one into dangerous deep water. Think of the

dreadful things that might happen if Johnny should borrow your family car, take it out and get in an accident. Your family may be fond of Johnny, even approve of him as your steady date, but a car is a car, and damage that runs into hundreds of dollars cannot be laughed off.

Far better is it to get along with what you've got, making the best of things and being responsible for your own property. Perhaps there will be times when you are asked to lend something. Okay, go ahead if you feel you should. Such requests are often difficult to turn down from friends. But, on the other hand, just because such requests are difficult to turn down, don't make your friends' lives complicated by asking them to lend you their things.

If, as will happen, you do lend something that gets broken, be nice about it, help put the borrower at ease. Smooth over the incident. If the person offers to pay, let him make amends if he insists, but always make sure that you don't demand payment. Often the other person is not in a position to do so. He already feels badly; your adamant position only makes him feel more miserable and helps nothing.

Do, when you have borrowed something (on strict necessity only), return the article in good condition. If clothing, make certain it is clean and fresh. If a book, no torn, dog-eared pages, please. Always thank the lender graciously and try to return the favor with a little gift — maybe just a flower or a hankie tucked in the package when you take it back.

To Remember

1. Give gifts that are carefully and thoughtfully chosen, not just "any old thing."
2. Don't give expensive presents to boys, even your best steady.
3. Remember that money does not determine the value of a gift.
4. Be sure to give a shower gift in keeping with the theme of the party.
5. Weekend visits always require a "house" present, given to the hostess.
6. Wrap gifts prettily and neatly.
7. Be gracious and sincere in your thanks for a gift.
8. Never borrow, if you can possibly avoid it.

20

The Table—
At It and On It

1. TABLE MANNERS

Good manners at the table begin at the beginning, right from the minute you set foot in the dining room. Take your chair quietly. Young people should wait for their elders.

The napkin belongs on your lap — not up under your ears like a bib, or on the floor like a dust mop. If you sit still, you'll find it won't wander.

Use your knife and fork gently. It is customary to hold the fork in your right hand, transferring it to your left to cut meat. You may, of course, keep the fork in your left hand, but if you do, hold it prongs down. In any case, remember that knives and forks are not instruments of torture, but refined implements to make eating neat and tidy.

When you have finished with your knife and fork, place them side by side toward the upper right half of the plate. Turn the knife blade in. Never leave silver sprawled haphazardly about your plate.

Make your actions small and precise. Elbows should stick close to the body.

Backs are supposed to be straight. Only the Romans reclined at the table, and they had couches, not our modern upright chairs.

Spoons are used only for soup, coffee, some first courses (such as fruit cup or grapefruit) and some desserts. They are not used during the main course, not even for the elusive pea. Never rattle a spoon around in a cup, and always place it on the saucer or edge of the plate.

By and large, since the invention of flat silver, fingers have taken a back seat. There are, however, some foods that may be eaten with your fingers. These are sandwiches, corn on the cob, radishes, olives, celery and the like, potato chips and artichokes. Fruits, such as apples, bananas and pears, are usually eaten in the hand, but they may be eaten with knife and fork. When it comes to a decision as to whether or not you should lift a finger, do as those about you are doing. At home follow family custom. Dining out, watch what your hostess does.

Never spit out seeds. Remove them from your mouth with a spoon.

Never talk with your mouth full.

Four Important DON'Ts in Table Manners

Soup in a handled cup may be drunk like a beverage. But use only *one* hand!

Remember that when food is pased by a waitress, it is offered on your left. Plates are taken away from the right.

It is considered polite to take something of everything offered. To refuse a course makes a hostess feel that you do not like what she has prepared for you. This wrecks havoc with diets, but cements friendships. And eat at least one mouthful, it won't kill you, and there is no law against leaving the rest on your plate.

Wait for your hostess to begin before you pitch in.

Don't get up from the table until everyone has finished. This means at home as well. If you have a date, a live one or a TV facsimile, ask permission to be excused. Never get up and go. If you must leave the table, excuse yourself as you do so.

Whenever you are in doubt as to what to do (if you are confronted with an unfamiliar food or a strange piece of silver), keep calm and watch what others do.

2. TABLE SETTINGS

Napkins go at the left of the plate.

Flat silver should be placed in order of use, beginning at the outside.

When salad is served for the main course, the dinner fork may be used.

Place all forks to the left of the plate, prongs up. Knives, blade in, and spoons go to the right.

At informal dinners, the dessert silver is usually put on the table at the beginning of the meal. For more formal service, the dessert silver is brought in with the dessert plate. The tiny after dinner coffee spoon, used with a demi-tasse cup, is placed on the saucer of the cup.

Water glasses should be placed just above the point of the knife. The bread and butter plate, with the butter spreader, is put above the fork.

Service plates are used for formal dinners and luncheons. They are on the table through the soup course; then they are removed.

It helps when you are planning a party to have some pointers on food and refreshments. Here are some of my own favorites — all tried and true. Easy to fix, too.

3. SUGGESTED MENUS FOR TEEN-AGE PARTIES

1. *Friday or Saturday night party at your house.* Serve coke and/or ginger ale early in the evening, accompanied with pretzels, potato chips and peanuts. The real food comes later, such as:

Ham and cheese sandwiches
Cream cheese and olive sandwiches
Tuna fish salad sandwiches
Peanut butter and jelly sandwiches
A fancy party cake and cookies, or
Ice cream and cake
More coke and ginger ale

2. *Sorority or club meeting (girls only).*
Fruit punch (mix together and ice in refrigerator 1 can frozen orange juice prepared according to directions, 1 can frozen grape juice (ditto), 1 can regular unsweetened grapefruit juice).
Cake or eclairs or cream puffs. (Sometimes the ones from a local bakery make a big hit.)
Cream cheese and olive, or cream cheese and jelly sandwiches instead of cake, if your crowd's on a diet.

3. *After sledding or skating party at your house.*
Lots of *hot* chocolate or cocoa for the frozen crew. Top this off with a dab of whipped cream or marshmallow.
Instant coffee or tea for non-cocoa drinkers.
Broiled cheese and bacon sandwiches (1 slice of bread, 2 slices American or Swiss cheese, 2 slices partially cooked bacon. Place in the broiler till cheese is melted.)
Cookies — a huge plateful of 'em.

4. *Barbecue in your backyard.*
Tomato juice cocktail *or* coke
Potato chips, pretzels
Hot dogs with toasted rolls
Hamburgers with toasted rolls
Sliced cheese — for those who go in for cheeseburgers
French fried potatoes — get frozen ones to be heated in the oven
Tossed green salad with lots of tomatoes in it

Watermelon *or* ice cream
Cookies
Iced tea or coffee

5. *When the gang drops in during Christmas holidays.*
Christmas punch (1 can frozen orange juice, thawed; 2 tablespoons each of lemon and lime juice; 1 tablespoon corn syrup; 2 cups water; $\frac{3}{4}$ cup pineapple juice; 1 cup ginger ale; dash of salt)
Hot walnuts, right out of the oven
Big fresh apples

6. *Halloween doin's.*
White slabs of ice cream (to look like tombstones)
Oval cookies with white icing (to look like ghosts' heads)
Round cookies with orange icing (to look like jack-o-lanterns)
Coke or ginger ale
or just a plain cider and doughnut party

7. *Luncheon (girls only).*
a. In the good old summer time:
Tomato salad
Chicken salad on lettuce leaves
Potato chips
Carrot sticks, radishes, sliced tomatoes
Hot rolls and butter
Ice cream and cookies
Iced tea or coffee, or milk
b. When it's cold outside:
Heated tomato juice
Chicken à la king in patty shells
Peas
Tossed green salad
Hot rolls and butter
Ice cream and cookies or ice cream cake
Hot coffee and milk
Note: After-dinner mints always make a hit!

One place setting for a Formal Dinner
Shows correct placing of china, silverware and glassware.

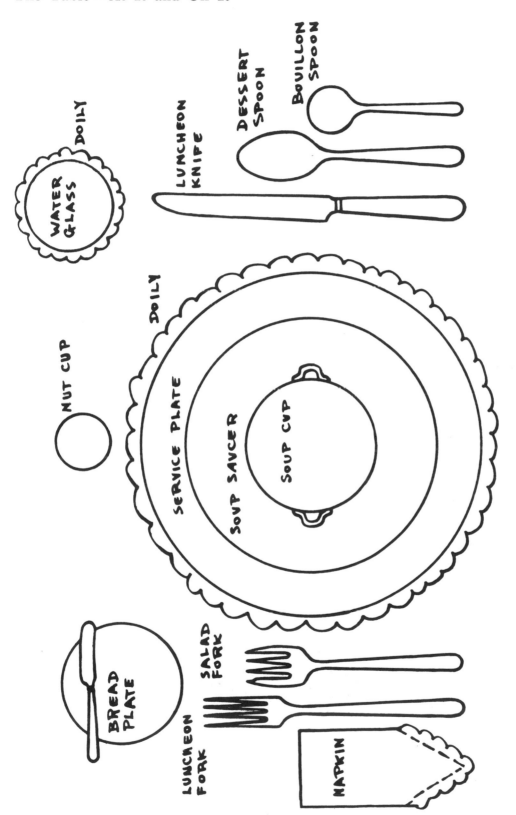

Arrangement of the china, silverware and glassware for each place at
a Formal Luncheon

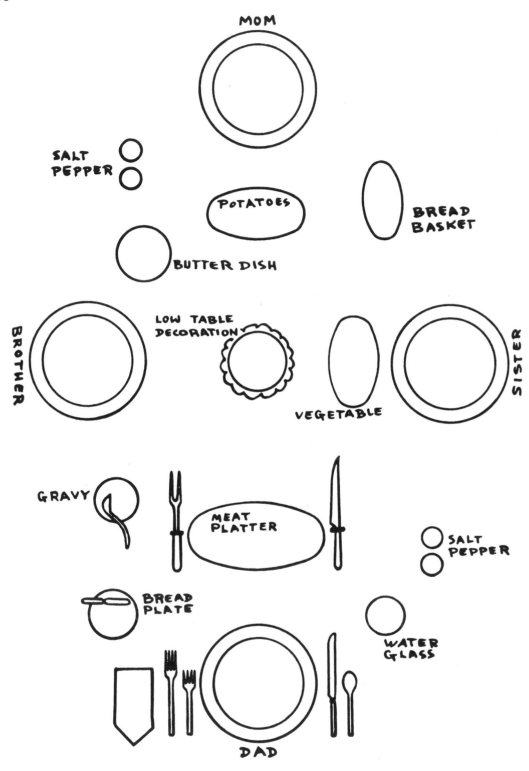

MOM

SALT
PEPPER

POTATOES

BREAD
BASKET

BUTTER DISH

BROTHER

LOW TABLE
DECORATION

VEGETABLE

SISTER

GRAVY

MEAT
PLATTER

SALT
PEPPER

BREAD
PLATE

WATER
GLASS

DAD

Table setting for home service without service of maid
Everybody has a napkin, silver, bread and butter plate
and water glass, as shown at Dad's place.

21

Personality

"*It's a date.*"

"*See you at eight then.*"

It's as easy as that. You're all set. You're going out to have fun, see a show or drop in to dance somewhere. Only sometimes it doesn't work out that way. Sometimes the phone doesn't ring, sometimes the boys don't stop by your house on the way home after school, sometimes the girls don't tell you about a slumber party they're planning. Sometimes nothing happens, and those sometimes are the worst times any girl can have.

Such times occur even in the lives of the

best of us, times when the social whirl slows to a standstill and life becomes a dreary round of music lessons and movies with the family. However, don't let these bad times get you down. If your steady beau, Johnny, has not called you in a week; if your best friend, Sally, suddenly starts walking home with another girl; if the prom is only two weeks away and you still haven't been bid, don't fold up.

Look the facts square in the face. Maybe this social slump has come about because of your own behavior. Maybe you've been too sure of yourself lately. Maybe you told Johnny that he was getting to be a bore; maybe you told a secret about Sally you swore you would never tell; maybe you acted as if going to the prom was the very last thing you ever wanted to do.

On the other hand, perhaps this dismal droop in your social life isn't your fault at all. All of a sudden, Johnny just decides to be indifferent, Sally is working off a peeve, and the prom is just one of those horrors that happen. If that is the case and you are as innocent as a newborn babe, it still does no good to sulk. Sulking never helped anyone.

No matter why the phone has stopped ringing, you are not going to improve matters by sitting up nights devising devilish tortures for every person you consider has done you wrong. You will only get dark circles under your eyes and a nasty disposition to boot. You will only make the situation worse if you take a negative attitude, if you shrug your shoulders and say, "Well, after all, who cares?"

Basically somebody does care. You care. You care, because like everyone else on this planet you want to be liked, you want to be popular, you want to be a girl who gets around. You want to have a crowd to pal around with, a few exciting dates and at least one boy who thinks you are about the most terrific female ever. If you say that you don't, you are really only fooling yourself. You are certainly not fooling others.

If you say, "I don't care," and start putting that philosophy into practice, you will find that you start retreating from life. You will withdraw into a shell until people will have a hard time deciding whether you are truly you or just an oyster. Now oysters, no doubt, have a way of communicating with other oysters in spite of their forbidding exteriors, but human beings are differently constructed. Human ·beings talk only to people who are willing to talk with them in return. They will warm up only to people who show that they have warmth to respond. If you want to be a human being, and a

Johnny will come racing back, Sally will call you up for a coke and a confession and the phone will start ringing again like mad.

First of all, let me say that every girl can be attractive. "Oh," you say, "it's easy enough for you to talk, you're a model." Of course, you are right. I am a model. As I pointed out before, I was not born a model. I had to make the best of what I had, just as you are doing. I had to experiment. I had to discover what was most becoming to me, to find out what weight was suitable for my figure, to find out which way my hair looked the most flattering, to slick up my makeup and to improve my posture. Things were not always smooth sailing. I had my ups and my downs. There were times when my skirts fitted me like panty girdles. There were

popular human being, then you have to stop being an oyster and come out of your shell.

So when things go badly, you must decide not to retreat; you must attack. But you attack in a special way, not by going out and slugging the first person who comes along, not by getting into an argument with your mother (who, after all, has had nothing to do with your troubles); you attack by working out your displeasure in a determined effort to make yourself so doggoned attractive that

times when my face was as splotchy as an ink blotter. And there were times when my hair straggled all over my head.

But I learned how to put my best face and figure forward. I found out that being attractive was not so hard, and therefore I decided, as I explained to you in the beginning of this book, that because making the best of oneself was so easy I would share my knowledge with you. Now, before I have my final say, I want to stress one thing. Being pretty and attractive does help you to be popular, but being pretty and attractive does not and never can guarantee that you will be popular. There is another factor, a very important factor, and that is personality. Personality is that indescribable something that sets you off as a person. It is hard to explain but easy to recognize. You yourself know what it is when you say, "'Gee, that Jane Smith, she sure has personality." Or, "She's sure got it." What you are saying is that Jane sparkles, she's alive, she's way out of her shell, in fact, there's no shell there at all.

Jane is the kind of person people like to talk to, boys as well as girls. She warms up to everybody and she is interested in whatever they have to say. She will discuss with equal enthusiam last night's date or tomorrow's homework. But, at the same time, Jane will never pry into your personal affairs. She will not question you about this or that unless you ask her opinion. Jane is careful about what she says because she has learned that nasty words have a way of coming back like boomerangs. She may not like the smart aleck in math class (the one who always knows all the answers) any better than you do, but she keeps quiet about it. There may be a time, she knows, when that very smart aleck might be the only boy in the stag line.

Another aspect of Jane's personality is her desire to avoid bigotry. She is tolerant —she has respect for other people's beliefs, and she does not make fun of anyone who holds different opinions from hers. She keeps an open mind about complex questions of religion, politics, and such matters. She has her own feelings about these things, but she does not try to force them on others, nor does she think that those who differ are stupid. Because she is open-minded, she would try never to blackball anyone.

Blackball is a nasty word. When you say it it even tastes bad on the tongue. So it's a pity, then that too many of us think that it's the thing to do. Without so

much as a thought, one girl will rule another out of her club because she doesn't like the way she wears her hair or because she speaks with an accent. Jane, on the other hand, never bases her opinions on a girl's mannerisms or her family's car. Jane decides on the basis of fairness. Jane judges a girl on the girl's own merits.

But Jane is no goody-goody. She is just a popular girl. She acts in a friendly way, therefore she has friends. Naturally some of her friends are closer than others, and with these friends she feels more at ease. But she does not tie herself down to the narrow circle of her really close friends; she is a big enough person to know how to be pleasant to everybody, to say, "Hi," smile and go on.

One of the most important aspects of Jane's personality—the most important, in fact—is that her personality is all hers. It is not borrowed from a movie star, from a local college queen or from her mother. Jane is all Jane. Her personality is her own.

And just as Jane's personality is all her own, so is her appearance. She does not try to pattern her looks after someone else, no matter how beautiful the other person may be. Jane looks like herself. She has individuality.

Jane's individuality makes her memorable. You never think of her as that girl who looks like ———, you think of her as herself. On the other hand, Jane's individuality does not prevent her from following fashion trends. She adapts herself to what is new. When hair is short, so is hers, but cut to become her, not cut to look like a recent fashion ad. Still, Jane, in trying not to look like others, does not carry the attempt too far. She strives to strike a happy medium. She keeps in fashion, but she also keeps on looking like

herself. She has developed what is known as her own sense of style, for style is merely the sum total of what you wear and the way you wear it.

Jane knows that a stylish person is one who takes the best from each new fashion and fits it to herself. She does not swallow a new fashion whole, but adapts it to her own figure and personality.

Now there are girls, unlike Jane, who are always trying to look like somebody else. One year it is this movie star, the next year another. They concentrate so hard on being a carbon copy that their own features get smudged in the process. They never give themselves a chance to develop their own style because they are so busy copying somebody else's.

After all it is pretty wonderful to think that there is nobody in this entire world who looks exactly like you (unless you are an identical twin). You are unique. You may take a bit after your mother, you may have your father's eyes, but essentially you are you. And being you, you are all yours to make or break. You should be proud of that fact, so proud that it makes you want to get up and do the very best you can for yourself.

You will do the best you can if you get up the gumption to develop your own style, preserve your own personality and make like an individual. Now, of course, you cannot assert yourself all over the place. There are circumstances and customs that limit you. You are subject to the habits and ideas of the world you live in. Your parents, your school, your friends, your total environment combined with the exact point of time in which you live, all affect you.

These influences tend to integrate you into your community. By the way you look, talk and think you are identified as a modern American teen-ager, just as by the way she looked and behaved a Gibson Girl was identified as a young woman of the early 1900's. At the opening of a play, the author always designates the time and the place. He does this because without that knowledge his characters would be acting in a void, their actions would have no point of reference. Your point of reference is America today.

Within this framework you move, and when the framework changes you change along with it. Just think how many changes have taken place in America since 1900 and how many will take place before 2000. Every year, every month, things change, big things and little. The trick is in knowing how to adapt to changes and still maintain your own standards and your own individuality.

Most people adapt easily. No one wants to be a fuddy-duddy and be out of fashion. The trouble comes from the fact that some people adapt too easily. They are too readily shifted by every prevailing whim. These are the people who have not established their own personality—their own individuality. They are busy, busy copying everybody else. They are suffering from what I call a crowd complex.

You know what a crowd is: it's the bunch you go around with, your own special group of friends. The top crowd, and there is one in every school, usually sets the pace and the others follow in line. And inside that large circle of follow-the-leader, there are smaller circles, for it usually happens that the members of each group tend to do just what the most important person in their crowd does.

Take, for example, this situation: The Rah-Rahs (the big crowd) decide that it is smart to wear bright green sweaters. Pretty soon everybody is wearing bright green sweaters. There is nothing wrong in that, except the fact that on some people bright green is mighty unbecoming. Where the situation becomes dangerous is when the top crowd decides that it is smart to drink or to drive cars at seventy miles an hour on a dark winding road. Then those people who follow that lead are being foolish, for they are endangering their lives and happiness. They are sheep being led to the slaughter.

Now, chances are that you have come across situations like these more than once in your life. In fact, chances are that at one time or another you actually did something you knew to be wrong, but you excused yourself by saying, "Gee, Mom, the crowd does it." Well, let the crowd do it, but don't do it yourself. Develop your own standards and your own judgments. Learn to say "No" gracefully. Don't be afraid of declaring your own independence. Don't feel that you have to compromise your personal standards in order to be accepted as one of the bunch. If you know that the crowd intends to go out for a wild drive and you know that what they are planning is wrong, tell them that you can't come—that you have a headache, that your mother needs you in the house, that you have a baby-sitting appointment that you can't break. Get an excuse and then stick to it; don't weaken.

Admittedly, it is difficult to decide when to act differently from your crowd, but it is a decision that you must make if you want to become a person in your own right. You can no more become a well-rounded personality if you become a slave to crowd customs than you can be attractive in your own right if you pattern yourself after a movie star. If you are going to amount to a row of beans in this world, you have to start by setting up your own standards and sticking to them. And it need not be added, I hope, that such standards should be based on decency and good taste.

There are some crowd customs which it is fun for everyone to follow—things like everybody wearing one blue and one white sock, wearing club jackets and hats, or shaking hands in a special way. These are all sacred secrets and rites that set you off from other crowds and make yours different. Such things do nobody any harm and are fun. So do not misunderstand me. I know that a crowd is fun. I think that going with a group who knows you and whom you know in return makes life lots easier. You date the same boys, you plan your parties together, you sit in the same row in school (if you can), and you visit each other overnight and weekends. You learn a lot by discussing your problems together. I'm all for it.

What I am *not* for is letting a crowd get the better of you. I do not believe that a crowd should be the sole basis of your opinions, the sole judge of what you should wear and the sole jury about what you should do. Belong to your crowd, but be above it. Remember that you will never gain anyone's respect by being a rubber stamp. The girls you copy will resent it (even though they are flattered), and the boys will think that you are pretty dumb if you can't do something original on your own.

Do not underestimate a boy's intelligence. They may seem pretty stupid about some things—they may get their feet tangled on the dance floor or stumble on their tongues when talking to your parents, but they are smart enough to know that a girl who just follows the crowd hasn't got very much on the ball. They would rather date a girl who sets

the pace than one who just jogs along.

Be careful, though, how you set the pace. Don't get steamed up without knowing where you are going. Search your route cautiously, testing each way before you choose it. Try to be to yourself what a good suit is to your wardrobe: a constant classic that can be dressed up or down according to the occasion.

Maybe you ask, what has this all got to do with popularity? The answer is that popularity depends on your ability to get along with people, all kinds of people, and the better you learn to adjust to each situation the more easily you will make friends. You will find that you can make those adjustments more successfully if you have yourself well in hand. And the only way to get yourself in hand is to know yourself, to analyze yourself, to turn yourself inside out as you would an old pocketbook—shake out the dust and tidy up the contents.

I hope that this little book will have given you some insight into how to turn yourself out. I hope that you will see what you gain by putting your best self forward. I hope most of all that you will have enjoyed what you have read here. I did not write this book to scare you, to make you shun your mirror or run from your friends. I only wrote it to put down on paper all those small but helpful suggestions on how to make the most of oneself that I have learned as a model. I don't expect that all of them will apply to every single one of you. But I do hope that some of them will apply. If you find just one or two of them useful, then I will consider that perhaps I did not make a mistake when I switched momentarily from Betty Cornell, the model, to Betty Cornell, the author.

Teen-Age
Exercises

Just to limber up, and aid the waistline, stand with feet together, tummy tucked in; hold the arms high above your head and reach for the ceiling.

Keeping the knees straight and feet together, touch your toes ten to twenty times. This is an excellent exercise for muscle tone and to slim the waistline.

Here's another waist-cincher. Stand with feet apart, hand resting on your knee, other hand above the head; now reach, stretch, and pull first to the right—then to the left, about ten times to each side.

Now, for the hips, the old rocking chair. Sit with crossed feet, hands on knees; rock back and forth on those hips.

Now to flatten the tummy, resorting again to the boys' football practice. Lie on the floor and raise the feet to a 45-degree angle; now lower them, keeping the knees straight, ever so slowly to the count of ten. Feel it pull? Although I know this exercise hurts, it also helps.

Stay right on the floor in a sitting position, with hands behind for balance. We're ready to slim down your legs. Raise first the left leg, then the right, and slap, really beat those legs on the floor about fifty times.

How about those ankles? Stay right on the floor and raise first the right leg and circle the foot from the ankle, keeping the leg straight, a little circle to the right twenty times, and to the left twenty times; now the left leg.

What we're all striving for is a well-developed,
well-proportioned figure, straight shoulders, small
waist and hips, well-shaped legs, and thin ankles,
so you too can stand up—smile and be proud.

Teen-Age
Calorie Table

According to doctors' research, the average teen-age girl—YOU—needs 2,000 calories every day. So, here's a calorie table designed especially for you. You'll be able to add them up yourself.

But again I stress: BEFORE YOU START DIETING TO GAIN OR LOSE, CONSULT YOUR FAMILY DOCTOR.

BEVERAGES

	No. of Calories
Milk, 1 cup	166 c
Milk shakes, 1 cup with ice cream	300 c
Malted milks, 1 cup with ice cream	300 c
Coca Cola, 1 cup	100 c
Gingerale, 1 cup	100 c
Carbonated drinks (lime, root beer, etc.), 1 cup	100 c
Lemonade, 1 cup	75 c
Orangeade, 1 cup	100 c
Coffee, black	none
Coffee, with 2 tablespoons cream and 2 teaspoons sugar	100 c
Tea, black	none
Tea, with milk and sugar	100 c
Chocolate milk, ½ cup	100 c
Orange juice (juice of 1 orange)	100 c
Tomato juice, 1 cup	50 c
Pineapple juice, ¾ cup	100 c
Grape juice, ⅔ cup	100 c
Apple cider, 1 cup	100 c
Grapefruit juice, 1 cup	100 c

BREADSTUFFS

White bread, 1 slice plus ⅛" slice of butter	100 c
Rye, 1 slice plus ⅛" slice of butter	100 c
Whole-wheat, 1 slice plus ⅛" slice of butter	100 c
Cinnamon buns, 1 small	100 c
Coffee cake, 1 small piece	100 c
Plain muffins, 1 medium	100 c
Bran muffins, 1 medium	75 c
Waffles, 1, 6" in diameter, without butter and syrup	250 c
Pan and griddle cakes, 1, 4½" in diameter	100 c
Baking powder biscuits, 1 medium	95 c
Melba toast, 2, ½" slices	100 c

(Mild toasting of any bread, white, rye or whole-wheat does not change the caloric value of the bread, so don't heap on the butter after you've toasted your bread, thinking you've cut down on some of the calories.)

Rye Krisp, 2, ½″ slices . . . . ·50 c

BREAKFAST CEREALS

Shredded wheat, 1 N.B.C. biscuit . . . . 25 c
Wheaties, ¾ cup . . . . 100 c
All-Bran, ½ cup . . . . 100 c
Bran flakes, ¾ cup . . . . 95 c
Puffed rice, 1 cup . . . . 105 c
Grape-Nuts, 3 tablespoons . . . . 55 c
Oatmeal, ⅓ cup . . . . 100 c
Farina, ¾ cup . . . . 100 c

(Of course milk or cream and sugar added are all extra calories.)

SANDWICHES
(Made with Two Slices of Bread)

Peanut butter . . . . 300 c
Tuna fish . . . . 300 c
Chopped egg . . . . 300 c
Sliced chicken . . . . 300 c
Hamburger . . . . 300 c
Cheeseburger . . . . 300 c
Ham . . . . 300 c
Cottage cheese . . . . 200 c
American cheese . . . . 300 c
Swiss cheese . . . . 300 c
Cream cheese . . . . 300 c

(Note: If mayonnaise is used add 100 calories extra for each tablespoon. Also, if butter is used, remember 1 square of butter has 50 calories.)

BETWEEN-MEAL NIBBLING, SNACKS, AND DESSERTS

CANDIES:

Caramels, 1 . . . . 100 c
Chocolate creams, 1 large . . . . 100 c
Chocolate fudge, 1″ cube . . . . 100 c
Jelly beans, 6 to 7 . . . . 50 c
Peanut brittle, 2, ½″ square . . . . 100 c
Chocolate mints, 2 . . . . 100 c

Popcorn, sugared, 1/2 cup . . . . 100 c
Candy bars, 1, 5¢ plain . . . . 250 c

ICE CREAM:

Plain vanilla, 1/4 cup . . . . 100 c
Plain chocolate, 1/2 cup . . . . 250 c
Plain strawberry, 1/2 cup . . . . 150 c
Plain coffee, 1/2 cup . . . . 200 c
Ice cream sodas, 1 glass . . . . 300 c
Hot fudge sundaes . . . . 400 c
Butterscotch sundaes . . . . 375 c

NUTS, TIDBITS:

Peanuts, 1/3 cup or 9 large nuts . . . . 100 c
Cashews, 10 nuts . . . . 100 c
Potato chips, 9 . . . . 100 c
French fried potatoes, 1/2 cup . . . . 150 c
Pretzels . . . .
Peanut butter, 1 tablespoon . . . . 100 c
Plain popcorn . . . .

CAKES:

Devil's food . . . . 200 c
Angel food cake, 3" x 2" x 2" . . . . 100 c
Plain white cake, small piece . . . . 100 c
Doughnuts, 1/3" in diameter . . . . 200 c
Chocolate layer cake . . . . 100 c
Cup cake, 1 small . . . . 100 c
Sponge cake, 3" triangle . . . . 200 c
Pound cake, 2" x 2" x 1/4" . . . . 100 c
Fruit cake, 2" x 2" x 1" . . . . 300 c

COOKIES AND CRACKERS:

Graham crackers, 2, 1/2" square . . . . 100 c
Oatmeal cookies, 2 . . . . 100 c
Soda crackers, 3, 2" square . . . . 50 c
Chocolate cookies, 3 . . . . 50 c
Tollhouse cookies, 2 . . . . 100 c
Butter cookies, 2 . . . . 100 c
Macaroons, 1, 1/2" in diameter . . . . 100 c
Vanilla wafers, 4 . . . . 100 c
Brownies, 1 . . . . 100 c
Gingersnaps, 4 . . . . 100 c
Wholewheat wafers, 1 . . . . 14 c
Chocolate-covered graham crackers, 2 . . . . 150 c

PIES AND PASTRIES:

Apple, ⅛ pie . . . . 350 c
Apricot, ⅛ pie . . . . 350 c
Berry, ⅛ pie . . . . 350 c
Custard, ⅛ pie . . . . 150 c
Lemon meringue, 4″ section . . . . 250 c
Mince, 3″ section . . . . 250 c
Pumpkin, ⅛ pie . . . . 150 c

PUDDINGS:

Bread pudding, ½ cup . . . . 100 c
Brown Betty, ¼ cup . . . . 100 c
Chocolate, ½ cup . . . . 300 c
Custard, ½ cup . . . . 150 c
Floating island, ⅓ cup . . . . 100 c
Jello, ½ cup . . . . 100 c
Junket, ½ cup . . . . 100 c
Prune whip, ½ cup . . . . 100 c
Rice custard, ¼ cup . . . . 150 c

(So, you heavyweights, when you're hungry for a snack, look back here first, and turn around and grab a piece of fruit, and just the reverse for you girls who weigh 10 pounds less than a straw hat, you reverse and dive into a large dish of high calorie pudding or a piece of that luscious chocolate cake.)

GRAVIES AND SAUCES

Catsup, chili sauce, 2 tablespoons . . . . 50 c
Cream sauce, 2¼ tablespoons . . . . 100 c
Hollandaise, 2 tablespoons . . . . 150 c
Meat gravy, 3 tablespoons . . . . 50 c
Cranberry sauce, ½ cup . . . . 150 c

SALAD DRESSINGS

French, 1 tablespoon (full) . . . . 100 c
Mayonnaise, 1 tablespoon . . . . 100 c
Roquefort, 1 tablespoon (full) . . . . 100 c
Thousand Island, 2 tablespoons . . . . 150 c
Miracle Whip, 1 tablespoon . . . . 100 c
Vinegar . . . . none

SUGARS

Brown, 4 teaspoons . . . . 50 c
White, granulated, 5 teaspoons . . . . 100 c
Cubes, 4 large . . . . 50 c
Powdered, 2 tablespoons . . . . 100 c

VEGETABLES

Asparagus, fresh, 18 pieces, 3″ long . . . . 50 c
Baked beans, ⅓ cup . . . . 100 c
String beans, 1⅓ cup . . . . 50 c
Lima beans, ½ cup . . . . 100 c
Beets, ⅔ cup . . . . 100 c
Broccoli, ¾ cup . . . . 50 c
Brussel sprouts, 1⅓ cup . . . . 50 c
Cabbage, boiled, 1⅔ cup . . . . 50 c
Carrots, 1 cup . . . . 50 c
Cauliflower, 2 cups . . . . 50 c
Celery, raw, 2 stalks . . . . 7 c
Corn on the cob, 1 car, 8″ long . . . . 100 c
Cucumbers, 1, 5″ long . . . . 10 c
Kale, 1 cup . . . . 50 c
Lettuce, 2 leaves . . . . 6 c
Olives, green, 5 large . . . . 50 c
Olives, ripe, 6–7 . . . . 100 c
Onions, raw, 2, 2″ in diameter . . . . 50 c
Onions, creamed, ⅓ cup . . . . 100 c
Peas, canned, ⅔ cup . . . . 50 c
Peas, fresh, ⅔ cup . . . . 100 c
Peppers, green, 1 . . . . 15 c
Potatoes, baked, 1 small . . . . 100 c
Potatoes, boiled, 1 medium . . . . 100 c
Potatoes, fried, ½ cup . . . . 100 c
Sweet potatoes, ½ medium . . . . 100 c
Sauerkraut, 1⅓ cup . . . . 50 c
Spinach, 1½ cup . . . . 50 c
Succotash, ¾ cup . . . . 200 c
Tomatoes, canned, 1 cup . . . . 50 c
Tomatoes, fresh, 2 small . . . . 50 c
Water cress, ½ cup . . . . 6 c

FRUITS

FRESH:

Apples, 1, 3" in diameter	100 c
Bananas, 1 medium	100 c
Cantaloupe, ½, 5" in diameter	50 c
Grapes, 20–25	100 c
Grapefruit, ½	50 c
Honeydew melon, ⅓	100 c
Orange, 1 medium	100 c
Peaches, 1 medium	50 c
Pears, 1, 3" long	50 c
Pineapple, ⅔ cup diced	50 c
Plums, 2, 2½" long	50 c
Raspberries, 1 cup	50 c
Strawberries, 1 cup	50 c
Tangerines, 2, 2" in diameter	50 c
Watermelon, 1 slice	100 c

CANNED:

Applesauce, ⅜ cup	100 c
Apricots, 5 halves	100 c
Fruit salad, ¾ cup	100 c
Grapefruit, ½ cup	50 c
Peaches, 3 halves	150 c
Pears, 3 halves	100 c
Pineapple, 2 slices	150 c
Plums, 3	100 c
Raspberries, ¾ cup	150 c
Strawberries, ¾ cup	150 c

(The calorie figures above are for fruit packed in medium syrup. When the fruit is packed in heavy syrup add an extra 50 calories per tablespoon of juice.)

EGGS, MEAT, POULTRY, AND FISH

EGGS:

Boiled, or poached, 1 large	70 c
Fried, 1 small	100 c
Omelet (2 eggs)	200 c
Scrambled, 2	200 c

BEEF:

Corned, 4″ x 3″ x ⅜″ . . . . 200 c
Liver, 3″ x 3″ x ⅜″ . . . . 100 c
Pot roast, 3″ x 3″ x 2″ . . . . 150 c
Prime rib roast, 1 slice 5″ in diameter . . . . 200 c
Ground round patty, broiled, 2½″ in dia. ¾″ thick . . . . 100 c
Sirloin steak, broiled, 3″ x 2″ x 2″ . . . . 200 c
Stew with vegetables, 6 tablespoons . . . . 100 c
Tongue, 2 slices . . . . 100 c

LAMB:

Chops, broiled, 2 small . . . . 200 c
Roast leg of lamb, 2 slices . . . . 200 c

PORK:

Bacon, broiled, crisp 2 slices, 7″ long . . . . 50 c
Ham, 4″ in diameter x ⅛″ . . . . 100 c
Chop, broiled, ¼ lb. . . . . 200 c
Roast, ¼ lb. . . . . 200 c
Bologna, 1 slice, 3″ in diameter . . . . 100 c
Frankfurter, 2, 7″ long . . . . 300 c

VEAL:

Cutlet, broiled, 2 small . . . . 200 c
Roast veal, 2 slices, 4″ x ¼″ . . . . 150 c

POULTRY:

Chicken, broiled, ½ small . . . . 100 c
Roast chicken, 2 slices, 4″ x 2″ x ¼″ . . . . 100 c
Roast duck, 3″ x 3″ x ¼″ . . . . 250 c
Turkey, breast, or other white meat, 4″ x 3″ x ¼″ . . . . . . 100 c

FISH:

Bluefish, 2″ x 2″ x 1″ . . . . 100 c
Codfish, 2″ x 3″ x 1″ . . . . 50 c
Mackerel, 2″ x 4″ x 2″ . . . . 150 c
Salmon, 3″ x 4″ x ¾″ . . . . 200 c
Swordfish, 1 steak . . . . 250 c
Tuna, ½ cup . . . . 100 c
Shrimp, 10 medium . . . . 100 c

(The above list contains most of the foods generally eaten by the average high school teen-age girl.)

Index